CONTENTS

BREADS

DESSERTS

VEGETABLES AND SALADS

MAIN DISHES

DRESSINGS AND SAUCES

Cooks' Notes
Kitchen Hack
Resources .
About the Au
Index . . . . .

ACKNOWLEDGMENTS

"Let's do a cookbook!" It sounded so easy. But having written a number of books, we can say without reserve that an endeavor like this takes an all-star cast. There were many more people involved in this cookbook than in our more traditional books.

The first group involved was the H.I.M. Board. After our proposal of a simple black and white, no-pictures cookbook, the discussion turned lively. The final encouragement was for us to produce a cookbook with color photos, scripture, historical stories, testimonials, and original artwork—and the rest, as they say, is history.

The idea originated with Virginia, the master baker and head cook in the Friesen household and head cook for many functions. Virginia has an exceptional gift for meeting real needs of people and being the hands and feet of Jesus in the process. As James 2:16 says: "If one of you says to them, 'Go in peace; keep warm and well fed,' but does nothing about their physical needs, what good is it?"

The next step was working with Barbara Steele, our editor, formatter, and dear friend, who has turned all our literary dreams into reality instead of nightmares. Her ability to understand design concepts and new software applications and her patience with our lack of that ability have been a true gift to us. Her husband, Guy, is the final proofreader, whose expertise and insights have been invaluable. We can truly say this book would never have come to fruition without Guy and Barbara.

In the early stages of the development of the cookbook, our dear friend Wendy Turney (of "I wish I had made him more Jello" fame from the opening chapter of *The Marriage App*) came to visit us in Boston. Wendy is an artist, and as we talked together about the book, we asked her about doing some watercolors for the cover. Soon we expanded the request to include the section pages, and then we boldly made additional specialized requests, such as "a painting of a pumpkin on this page would be great!" The artistic rendering of the book is really due to Wendy.

But then Wendy said, "My daughter Emily has a company that does incredible design work. I'll ask her for a little time." It turned into a lot. We are so appreciative of Emily Owen and her company, Wiley-Valentine, for all their assistance.

HOSTED BY

PAUL & VIRGINIA FRIESEN

The Family Table

COOKBOOK

GREAT RECIPES   ORDINARY INGREDIENTS   LASTING MEMORIES

The Family Table
© 2021 by Paul and Virginia Friesen.

Cover design: Emily Owen, www.wileyvalentine.com
Photos: Paul and Virginia Friesen
Watercolor illustrations: Wendy Turney, dsn4u@att.net
Production: Barbara Steele
Copy editing: Guy Steele

ISBN: 978-1-936907-15-1

Scripture quotations on pages 3, 6, 11, 37, 40, 63, 74, 77, 95, 98, and 101 are taken from the Holy Bible, New International Version®, NIV® Copyright ©1973, 1978, 1984, 2011 by Biblica, Inc.® Used by permission. All rights reserved worldwide.

Scripture quotations on pages 106 and 109 are from The ESV® Bible (The Holy Bible, English Standard Version®), copyright © 2001 by Crossway, a publishing ministry of Good News Publishers. Used by permission. All rights reserved.

All italics in quotations of Scripture have been added by the authors.

Published by Home Improvement Ministries.
For information on other H.I.M. resources, visit www.HIMweb.org/books
or contact:
Home Improvement Ministries
213 Burlington Road, Suite 101-B
Bedford, MA 01730
E-mail inquiries: info@HIMweb.org
Website: www.HIMweb.org

01/05-21TPS1500

WHEN HE WAS AT
THE TABLE WITH THEM,

He took bread
and gave thanks

LUKE 24:30

As for the recipes themselves, so many friends shared these with us. There are too many to name, but we could not have done this without your input.

Sorting through the recipes brought up vivid memories surrounding past meals and those who *really* seemed to enjoy certain offerings. And that is where the testimonials came from that you'll find scattered through this book.

I, Paul, am writing the acknowledgments, but Virgina is really the one who has cooked, baked, developed recipes, and written anecdotes about many of the offerings in the book. And Virginia has really been the one creating the memories surrounding so many of these cooked or baked items.

Our three girls didn't fall far from the tree. We have so appreciated their support for this project. Most of all, we celebrate that they, too, are using the family table as an avenue for sharing Christ.

Our grandkids, Brandon, Ana, Nathan, Micah, and Rachel, have made cooking and baking even more fun—and a bit messier—and we have loved every minute of it.

And finally, the scriptures that have inspired us to offer simple hospitality. None of this, including our very lives, would be possible without the love, mercy, and sacrifice of the Lord Jesus. His Word is filled with references to His extension of hospitality: breaking bread, feeding the hungry, eating with sinners, and inviting those on the highways and byways to come eat with Him.

The greatest meal He will host—to which we all are invited—is the Marriage Supper of the Lamb, when those who call Him Lord will feast together in Heaven.

May God use this book to encourage many to use their table to point others to *His* Table, where we will never thirst again or be hungry any longer.

Paul Friesen, Director
Home Improvement Ministries

WELCOME

Is there anything more central to the experience of family life than the family table? It is the place where faith is expressed in giving thanks, where traditions are celebrated as passed-down-through-the-generations recipes are shared, where community is forged as daily "high and lows" are revealed, where serving is demonstrated, and where family values and ethos are on display.

The recipes collected here in *The Family Table* are "tried and true" family favorites, representing three generations of cooks who range from neophytes to self-avowed "foodies." Almost all are imbued with history, encompassing family legends and folklore, failures and successes, but most importantly, they have been the vehicle for carrying love, care, and sustenance to friends, neighbors, and "angels unaware" for decades.

Years ago I served as the Food Service Director for a Christian camp. We were committed to loving our campers well by serving satisfying, delicious, homemade food, believing that if they were well loved in the dining hall, they'd be more open to the gospel message of God's great love for them.

We still believe that true hospitality opens the door for the gospel message. Rosaria Butterfield's profound book *The Gospel Comes with a House Key* develops the gospel heart of hospitality consistent with the vision of *The Family Table*. Any time we practice hospitality (the focus of which is *serving* others, versus *entertaining*, the focus of which is impressing others), we are engaging in Kingdom work. Building community. Experiencing fellowship. Celebrating God's good gifts of food, taste, smell, and pleasure.

Our culture has exchanged the family table for meals on the run, front-row dining in view of the TV, individualized meal plans, or microwavable servings for one. Our hope is that this compilation of our favorite recipes will be helpful as you affirm the goodness and potential of the family table, or establish it as the standard for your family.

We invite you to sort through this cookbook, try the recipes that have warmed our hearts and homes, and join us in making memories and building traditions with your families and friends, as we have with ours. We pray that God meets you there as He has for us, for generations.

From the heart of our kitchen to yours,
Virginia Friesen

Bread

A GIFT OF LOVE

Then Jesus declared, "I am the bread of life.
Whoever comes to me will never go hungry" —John 6:35

CORNBREAD

SERVES	PREP	READY IN
6-8	15 minutes	40 minutes

Nothing like hot-out-of-the-oven cornbread, served with butter and honey and accompanied by a steaming bowl of chili or a rack of BBQ ribs!

INGREDIENTS

- **2** eggs
- **¼ cup** honey (or maple syrup)
- **2 cups** milk
- **1⅓ cups** cornmeal
- **1½ cups** flour
- **2 Tbsp** baking powder
- **1 tsp** salt
- **6 Tbsp** butter, melted

STEPS

- Preheat oven to 425°F and spray a 9" x 13" pan.
- Beat eggs until light, then add honey and milk.
- In separate bowl, combine cornmeal, flour, baking powder, and salt.
- Gradually stir dry ingredients into wet.
- Add melted butter and stir briskly.
- Pour into prepared pan and bake for 20 minutes or until done. Cut into ~3" squares (3 x 5 in pan).
- Serve hot with butter and honey.

EASY WHITE BREAD

MAKES
2 loaves

PREP
30 minutes

READY IN
3 hours

INGREDIENTS

2 Tbsp yeast

½ cup lukewarm water

2½ tsp salt, divided

2 Tbsp sugar

2 cups milk

5½ cups flour, divided

2 Tbsp butter, melted

additional melted butter, for
   brushing tops of loaves

STEPS

- In large bowl, dissolve yeast in lukewarm water.

- Stir in **1 tsp** salt, sugar, and milk, then gradually blend in **3 cups** of flour.

- Let this "sponge" mixture rise for 1 hour.

- Mix in **1½ tsp** salt and the melted butter.

- Work in approximately **2½ cups** flour, then turn out on a floured board and knead for 15 minutes.

- Shape into 2 loaves and place in greased 8½" x 4½" loaf pans. Let rise for about 45 minutes, or until doubled.

- Set oven to 350°F and bake for 35–45 minutes, until loaves are golden brown and sound hollow when thumped.

- Remove from oven and brush tops with butter.

OATMEAL BREAD

MAKES	PREP	READY IN
5 loaves	 30 minutes	3 hours

This dough also makes good rolls.

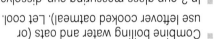

INGREDIENTS

1½ cups boiling water } see note below
1 cup rolled oats
2 cups lukewarm water
2 Tbsp yeast
¾ cup honey (or molasses)
3 Tbsp butter
2 tsp salt
8 cups flour (may be part whole wheat)

Note: you may replace the boiling water and rolled oats with 1½ cups leftover cooked oatmeal.

STEPS

- Combine boiling water and oats (or use leftover cooked oatmeal). Let cool.
- In 2-cup glass measuring cup, dissolve yeast in lukewarm water.
- In large mixing bowl, combine honey, butter, and salt, then stir in cooled oats and yeast mixture.
- Mix in flour. Add more flour as needed to make a medium-soft dough.
- Turn out onto floured surface and knead until smooth (about 15 minutes).
- Place dough in greased bowl; cover and let rise in a warm place until doubled in size (about 1 hour).
- Punch down. Form into five 1-lb round loaves, place on large greased baking tray, and let rise again ~45 minutes.
- Place risen loaves in oven and set to 350°F. Bake for 35 minutes or until loaves are golden brown and sound hollow when thumped.
- Transfer loaves to a wire rack to cool.

"With its soft rise, warm brown coloring, and mild yet nutty flavor, this hearty bread is heavenly. It has the perfect balance of softness and durability to hold up to the thickest of hungry-man sandwich fillings. I also love it toasted, with a smear of Virginia's homemade raspberry jam."
—Shahrzad S., MA

HONEY WHOLE WHEAT BREAD

MAKES
2 loaves

PREP
30 minutes

READY IN
3 hours

"For toast or sandwiches, this bread is a winner and worth every calorie consumed." —Dawn A., MA

INGREDIENTS

4 cups whole wheat flour, divided

2 Tbsp yeast

1 Tbsp salt

3 cups milk

½ cup honey

2 Tbsp oil

4-4½ cups white flour

melted butter, for brushing tops of loaves

STEPS

- In large bowl, combine **3 cups** whole wheat flour, yeast, and salt.

- In saucepan (or microwave), heat milk, honey, and oil just until warm (not hot).

- Pour the lukewarm liquid over the flour mixture and beat with an electric mixer for 3 minutes.

- Add **1 cup** whole wheat flour and **4 cups** white flour.

- Turn out onto floured surface and knead for 15 minutes, using additional white flour as needed, until dough is smooth and elastic.

- Place in greased bowl, cover with towel, and let rise until doubled.

- Punch down and shape into two loaves.

- Place in greased 9" x 5" loaf pans. Cover and let rise 40–45 minutes.

- Place risen loaves in oven and set to 350°F. Bake for 40–45 minutes, or until golden brown.

- Remove from oven and brush tops with butter. Let cool on racks.

CRANBERRY-WALNUT BREAD

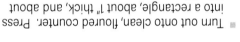		
MAKES	**PREP**	**READY IN**
3 loaves	25 minutes	3 hours

"The tartness of the cranberries and texture of walnuts makes this my family's favorite."
—Patty B., MA

INGREDIENTS

2 Tbsp yeast

2 cups lukewarm water

½ cup honey ⎱ may use all honey
¼ cup molasses ⎰ or all molasses

6 Tbsp olive oil

1½ tsp salt

2 tsp cinnamon

7-8 cups flour

1 cup chopped walnuts

1 cup dried cranberries

STEPS

- Dissolve yeast in lukewarm water in mixer bowl (we use a 6-quart KitchenAid).
- Add honey, molasses, oil, salt, and cinnamon. Mix with paddle.
- Add about half the flour and mix with paddle.
- Change to dough hook and gradually mix in the rest of the flour.
- Add additional flour as needed until the dough is smooth and elastic.
- Let rise in bowl for until doubled in size (~1 hour).

- Turn out onto clean, floured counter. Press into a rectangle, about 1" thick, and about 12" x 18".
- Sprinkle dough surface with walnuts and dried cranberries. Fold the dough in half, and then in half again.
- Divide into 3 equal pieces (about 1 lb each) and shape into rounds.
- Place on a large, greased baking tray and let rise until doubled, ~45-60 minutes.
- Place risen loaves in oven and set to 350°F. Bake for ~35 minutes or until done.
- Transfer loaves to a wire rack to cool.

BAKED BROWN BREAD

"Quintessential New England staple; great with soups and stews, or alone with butter."
—Laura L., VA

MAKES
2 loaves

PREP
15 minutes

READY IN
1 hour

Our family loves it when milk goes sour since it means either Baked Brown Bread or Cowboy Coffee Cake. Served with cream cheese, this bread could pass for dessert.

INGREDIENTS

1¼ cups brown sugar

2 eggs, beaten

¼ cup butter

2½ cups sour milk*

2½ tsp baking soda

½ cup dark molasses

5⅓ cups whole wheat flour

1 tsp salt

*To make sour milk, mix:

  2½ cups milk

  2½ Tbsp vinegar

Let sit for at least 5 minutes.

STEPS

- Preheat oven to 350°F. Spray two 1-lb loaf pans (7.5" x 3.25") with cooking spray.

- In large bowl, beat together brown sugar, eggs, and butter.

- In separate bowl, mix together sour milk, baking soda, and molasses.

- In third bowl, mix flour and salt.

- Alternating, add liquid mixture and flour mixture to egg mixture in large bowl.

- Pour batter evenly into the two loaf pans.

- Bake 45 minutes, or until done in center but not burned around the edges. (Rearrange pans in oven during baking, if necessary.)

- Remove loaves from pans and cool on wire rack before slicing.

HAMBURGER BUNS

MAKES	PREP	READY IN
12 buns	20 minutes	2½ hours

INGREDIENTS

1 Tbsp yeast

1¼ cups lukewarm milk

¼ cup butter, melted

2 Tbsp sugar

2 eggs, beaten

1 tsp salt

4-4½ cups flour (can be part whole wheat)

milk and sesame seeds (for tops—optional)

STEPS

- In large bowl, dissolve yeast in lukewarm milk.
- Add butter, sugar, eggs, and salt; mix well.
- Mix in 4 cups of flour.
- Knead on floured surface for 15 minutes (or use a KitchenAid mixer and its dough hook), adding in additional flour as needed to make a soft, satiny dough.
- Place in greased bowl. Cover and let rise until doubled.
- Punch down. Pinch off 3½-oz pieces of dough and shape into buns.
- Place buns 2" apart on greased baking tray. Cover and let rise 35-45 minutes.
- If desired: brush tops with milk and sprinkle with sesame seeds, onions, or "everything" spice before baking.
- Preheat oven to 375°F and bake for 15-20 minutes.
- Slice when cool.

"You'll never want a store-bought bun again!"
—Melissa C., OR

"These are absolutely the best rolls ever and our family favorite must-have at every holiday meal!"
—Wendy T., CA

MOM'S ROLLS

MAKES
24 rolls

PREP
20 minutes

READY IN
2 ½ hours

You could change the holiday main dish, but don't mess with the rolls!

Virginia's brother once ate a dozen by himself. Now in the third generation, the tradition continues. It's an incomplete holiday meal without these rolls.

These are unbeatable the day they're made, but if you're not going to eat them within a day or two, share them with a neighbor or freeze. They are also perfect for making little ham or turkey sandwiches with those leftovers.

INGREDIENTS

1 Tbsp yeast

¼ cup lukewarm water

1 cup milk

¼ cup sugar

¼ cup oil

1 tsp salt

1 egg, beaten

3 ½ cups flour

2 Tbsp butter, melted

STEPS

- Dissolve yeast in lukewarm water.
- Add milk, sugar, oil, and salt; mix well.
- Stir in beaten egg.
- Mix in flour. Add more flour as needed, but dough should be slightly sticky.
- Cover and let rise until doubled.
- Turn dough onto floured counter top and press into a large circle about ½–¾" thick.
- Brush dough with melted butter.
- Using a biscuit cutter (or a glass from the cupboard that's 2 ½" in diameter), cut 24 circles from the dough.
- Using a butter knife, make a crease in each circle, fold over, and place in prepared 9" x 13" pan: 3 across the 9" end, 8 down the 13" side.
- Let rise about 40 minutes.
- Preheat oven to 400°F and bake for 15 minutes.

FRESH APPLE MUFFINS

The New England tradition of apple picking inspired the development of this hard-to-resist recipe.

MAKES	PREP	READY IN
12 muffins	15 minutes	40 minutes

INGREDIENTS

1½ cups flour
½ cup sugar
2 tsp baking powder
¼ tsp baking soda
¼ tsp salt
1 tsp cinnamon
¼ tsp allspice
2 eggs
1 cup sour cream
¼ cup butter, melted
1 cup peeled, finely chopped apples

Topping:
½ cup chopped walnuts
¼ cup flour
3 Tbsp sugar
2 Tbsp cold butter
¼ tsp cinnamon

STEPS

- Preheat oven to 375°F. Spray a muffin pan with cooking spray or insert paper liners.
- Combine topping ingredients and mix until crumbly. Set aside.
- Mix together flour, sugar, baking powder, baking soda, salt, and spices.
- In separate bowl, mix eggs, sour cream, and melted butter.
- Combine wet and dry ingredients and stir in chopped apples.
- Pour batter evenly into muffin cups.
- Sprinkle on topping mixture.
- Bake for 20 minutes.

PUMPKIN STREUSEL MUFFINS

MAKES
12 muffins

PREP
20 minutes

READY IN
45 minutes

Don't throw those fresh pumpkins away!
Process them and make these melt-in-your-mouth muffins.

INGREDIENTS

½ cup butter, softened

1 cup brown sugar, packed

1 egg

1 cup freshly puréed pumpkin
(recipe, p. 41—*or use canned*)

¼ cup half-and-half

1¾ cups flour

1 tsp baking soda

½ tsp salt

2 tsp cinnamon

1 tsp ground ginger

½ tsp ground cloves

Streusel topping:

¼ cup flour

5 Tbsp sugar

2 Tbsp cold butter

2 tsp cinnamon

STEPS

- Preheat oven to 375°F. Spray a muffin pan with cooking spray or fill with paper liners.

- Cream butter and brown sugar.

- Add egg and mix together.

- Stir in pumpkin and half-and-half.

- In separate bowl, combine flour, baking soda, salt, and spices.

- Combine wet and dry ingredients and stir together.

- In separate bowl, mix streusel ingredients with fork or mixer until topping is the size of small peas.

- Pour batter evenly into muffin cups and sprinkle with streusel topping mixture.

- Bake 18–22 minutes or until done.

COWBOY COFFEE CAKE

SERVINGS	PREP	READY IN
2 dozen	15 minutes	45 minutes

This batter also makes nice muffins.

INGREDIENTS

2½ **cups** flour

2 **cups** brown sugar

½ **tsp** salt

⅔ **cup** butter

2 **tsp** baking powder

½ **tsp** baking soda

½ **tsp** nutmeg

½ **tsp** cinnamon

1 **cup** sour milk

2 eggs, beaten

"My favorite coffee cake! Always moist with the perfect amount of cinnamon and fresh nutmeg. Perfect for any occasion."
—Danielle B., TX

STEPS

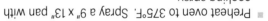

- Preheat oven to 375°F. Spray a 9" x 13" pan with cooking spray.
- Combine flour, brown sugar, salt, and butter; mix until crumbly.
- Reserve ½ **cup** of mixture for topping.
- To remaining mixture, sift together and add baking powder, baking soda, nutmeg, and cinnamon.
- In separate bowl, mix sour milk and beaten eggs, then add to flour mixture.
- Mix until dry ingredients are moistened.
- Pour into pan (or muffin tins) and sprinkle with reserved crumbs.
- Bake for 25-30 minutes.

"I love the rich, deep flavor of this coffee cake. I love it warm and buttered—or cold and unbuttered. It's just great any way."
—Melissa C., OR

RASPBERRY CREAM CHEESE COFFEE CAKE

SERVINGS
10–12

PREP
20 minutes

READY IN
1½ hours

"Is it breakfast? Dessert? It's every meal of the day 'til it's gone." —Kara M., MA

INGREDIENTS

2¼ cups flour

1 cup sugar, divided

¾ cup cold butter

½ tsp baking powder

½ tsp baking soda

¼ tsp salt

¾ cup sour cream

2 eggs, divided

1 tsp almond extract

8 oz cream cheese, softened

½ cup raspberry preserves

½ cup sliced almonds

STEPS

- Preheat oven to 350°F. Spray and flour bottom and sides of a 9" or 10" springform pan.

- Combine flour and **¾ cup** sugar; cut in butter to make coarse crumbs.

- Reserve **1 cup** of crumbs for topping.

- To remaining crumb mixture, add baking powder, baking soda, salt, sour cream, **1** egg, and almond extract. Blend well.

- Spread batter over bottom and ¼" thick for 2" up the sides of the pan.

- In separate bowl, mix cream cheese, **¼ cup** sugar, and **1** egg.

- Pour cream cheese mixture over batter.

- Carefully spoon raspberry preserves over cheese filling.

- Mix sliced almonds and reserved crumbs, then sprinkle over top.

- Bake for 45–55 minutes or until filling is set and crust is golden brown.

- Serve warm. Refrigerate leftovers.

BEST BLUEBERRY MUFFINS

MAKES	PREP	READY IN
12 muffins	20 minutes	45 minutes

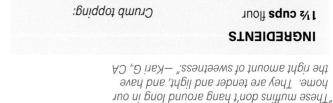

"These muffins don't hang around long in our home. They are tender and light, and have the right amount of sweetness." — Kari G., CA

INGREDIENTS

- **1½ cups** flour
- **¾ cup** sugar
- **½ tsp** salt
- **2 tsp** baking powder
- **⅓ cup** vegetable oil
- **1** egg, beaten
- **~⅓ cup** milk
- **1 cup** fresh or frozen blueberries

Crumb topping:

- **½ cup** sugar
- **⅓ cup** flour
- **¼ cup** butter, cubed
- **1½ tsp** cinnamon

STEPS

- Preheat oven to 375°F. Spray a muffin pan with cooking spray or fill with paper liners.
- In large bowl, combine flour, sugar, salt, and baking powder.
- Pour vegetable oil into a 1-cup glass measuring cup. Add beaten egg and enough milk to make 1 cup. Stir together well.
- Add liquid mixture to flour mixture, stirring just until moistened.
- Fold in blueberries.
- In separate bowl, mix topping ingredients with fork.
- Pour batter evenly into muffin cups and sprinkle with crumb topping mixture.
- Bake 20–25 minutes or until done.

LEMON RICOTTA BLUEBERRY PANCAKES

SERVES
4

PREP
15 minutes

READY IN
25 minutes

Serve these with blueberry sauce (see recipe on p. 106) and whipped cream for a special and delicious breakfast.

INGREDIENTS

1 cup flour

¼ cup sugar

1 tsp baking powder

¼ tsp salt

1 cup part-skim ricotta cheese

2 large eggs, separated

½ cup low-fat milk

2 Tbsp sugar

2 tsp grated lemon zest

1 tsp vanilla extract

1 cup fresh or frozen blueberries

STEPS

- Combine flour, sugar, baking powder, and salt.
- In separate bowl, whisk together ricotta, egg yolks, milk, sugar, lemon zest, and vanilla.
- Stir flour mixture into egg mixture until just combined.
- In a third bowl, beat egg whites until stiff.
- Gently fold the beaten egg whites into the batter.
- Fold in blueberries.

- Lightly oil a large non-stick griddle over medium heat.
- Pour heaping **¼ cup** batter onto griddle and spread to make a 4-inch pancake.
- Cook 3 minutes, or until edges are dry and bottom is golden.
- Flip pancake and cook 2–3 minutes longer or until lightly golden on both sides.
- Repeat with remaining batter, adjusting heat as needed.

"It's hard to improve on the marriage of fresh lemons and blueberries. These pancakes would turn any breakfast into a special occasion." —Derek J., VA

GRANDMA ESSIE'S WAFFLES

SERVES	PREP	READY IN
4-6	15 minutes	18 minutes

Leftover waffles (if there are any!) can be frozen and reheated in a toaster oven.

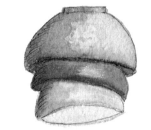

"A Saturday morning tradition growing up was waffles and smokies. Dad always made the waffles perfectly—a legacy we are all still trying to live up to."
—Kari G., CA

INGREDIENTS

1¾ cups flour

3 tsp baking powder

½ tsp salt

2 eggs, separated

1¾ cups milk

½ cup vegetable oil (we use olive oil)

STEPS

- Lightly oil waffle iron and preheat.
- In large bowl, combine flour, baking powder, and salt.
- In separate bowl, whisk egg yolks with milk and oil.
- In a third bowl, beat egg whites on high until stiff peaks form, about 1½ to 2 minutes.

- Add milk mixture to flour mixture and stir just until moistened.
- Gently fold in beaten egg whites.
- Pour ½ cup batter onto preheated waffle iron.
- Serve immediately with butter, syrup, powdered sugar, jam, peanut butter, whipped cream, and/or fresh fruit.

BAKED APPLE OATMEAL

SERVES
6

PREP
20 minutes

READY IN
1 hour

INGREDIENTS

2 ¼ cups old fashioned oats
2 Tbsp brown sugar
1 tsp baking powder
1 tsp cinnamon
¼ tsp salt
1 ¼ cups milk, any type
2 5- or 6-oz containers of yogurt
    (plain or vanilla)
1 large egg
2 Tbsp maple syrup
2 Tbsp butter, melted
1 tsp vanilla extract
2 cups thinly sliced apples
cinnamon sugar (*for topping*)

During the summer, we have made this with peaches or blueberries. Both work well!

STEPS

- Preheat oven to 350°F. Spray an 8" x 8" baking dish with cooking spray.

- Mix the oats, brown sugar, baking powder, cinnamon, and salt together in a medium bowl.

- In separate bowl, whisk together milk, yogurt, egg, maple syrup, melted butter, and vanilla extract.

- Scatter half the apple slices in the bottom of the prepared baking dish.

- Pour the oat mixture evenly on top.

"A hearty, warm way to wake up—tastes like home. One of our family favorites!" —Julie J., VA

- Pour the milk mixture on top and press to submerge all of the dry ingredients in the liquid.

- Arrange the remaining apple slices on top and sprinkle with cinnamon sugar (we use **2 tsp** sugar and **½ tsp** cinnamon).

- Bake for 35–40 minutes, until set. Let rest for 10 minutes before serving.

- Serve the oatmeal plain, or top it with a dollop of yogurt and/or maple syrup.

PUMPKIN WAFFLES

SERVES	PREP	READY IN
4	15 minutes	18 minutes

This makes 6 to 7 round waffles or 4 to 5 square waffles in a standard 4-square waffle iron.

INGREDIENTS

- ¼ **cup** light brown sugar
- **3 Tbsp** cornstarch
- 1¼ **cups** flour
- 1½ **tsp** baking powder
- ½ **tsp** salt
- **2 tsp** cinnamon
- **2 tsp** ground ginger
- ¼ **tsp** ground cloves
- ½ **tsp** freshly grated nutmeg*

- **2** large eggs, separated
- **1 cup** freshly puréed pumpkin (recipe, p. 41, or use canned)
- **1 cup** whole milk
- **4 Tbsp** butter, melted

*Note on nutmeg:
We are nutmeg lovers. You may substitute ground nutmeg.

STEPS

- Lightly oil waffle iron and preheat.
- In large bowl, combine brown sugar and cornstarch. Whisk to blend.
- Add remaining dry ingredients and mix together.
- In separate bowl, whisk egg yolks with pumpkin and milk.
- Pour butter into pumpkin mixture, whisking together as you pour.
- Add pumpkin mixture to the dry ingredients and stir until just combined (batter will be slightly lumpy).
- In a third bowl, beat egg whites on high until stiff peaks form, about 1½–2 minutes.
- Gently fold the beaten egg whites into the batter.
- Pour batter into preheated waffle iron.
- Serve hot off the iron with butter and warmed real maple syrup.

"Double the recipe, loosen your belt, and serve with warmed maple syrup and sizzling hot bacon." —Helen C., NY

GRANOLA

MAKES
25 cups

PREP
15 minutes

READY IN
1½ hours

Try topping yogurt and fresh fruit with ⅓ cup granola. Yum!

What to do as a head cook with hundreds of pounds of government surplus rolled wheat, rolled oats, peanuts, and honey? Beth Friesen Smith decided to make granola—and a time-tested tradition was born.

INGREDIENTS

16 cups rolled oats

4 cups unprocessed bran

2 cups raw sunflower seeds

2 cups coconut

3 cups nuts, chopped (*any combination you like*)

1 cup coconut oil (*or olive or any pure vegetable oil*)

1 cup brown sugar

1 cup honey

2 Tbsp vanilla extract

Optional additions **before** *baking:*

sesame seeds

wheat germ

rolled wheat

Optional additions **after** *baking:*

raisins

other dried fruits

STEPS

- Preheat oven to 300°F.

- In a very large bowl, mix together oats, bran, sunflower seeds, coconut, nuts, and any optional additions.

- In 2-qt saucepan over medium heat, stir together oil, brown sugar, and honey. Just as it comes to a boil, stir in vanilla.

- Pour wet ingredients over dry; mix well.

- Spread mixture onto large rimmed baking sheets. (You will need to bake just half of this at a time, two baking sheets at a time.)

- Bake for 1 hour, stirring every 30 minutes.

- Cool. If desired, stir in dried fruits.

Micah and Ana helping with the making of "Gigi Cakes" (aka Cinnamon Chip Scones). Always requested when Gigi is in town!

CINNAMON CHIP SCONES

 MAKES
24 scones

 PREP
25 minutes

READY IN
50 minutes

"A little bit of heaven here on earth!"
—Jordan P., MA

INGREDIENTS

Scones:

3 cups flour
½ cup sugar
5 tsp baking powder
1 tsp cinnamon
1 tsp salt
1 cup cold butter
¾–1 cup cinnamon chips
½ cup milk
1 egg

Frosting:

1½ cups powdered sugar
1 tsp cinnamon
2 Tbsp melted butter
1 Tbsp milk

STEPS

- Preheat oven to 375°F.
- In large bowl, mix flour, sugar, baking powder, cinnamon, and salt.
- Cut in butter until mixture resembles coarse crumbs.
- Stir in cinnamon chips.
- In separate bowl, mix milk and egg, then stir into flour mixture.
- Add more milk if needed to make the dough cohesive, but add *very* little, *very* slowly. Don't overmix!
- Divide dough into three 12-oz pieces and shape into balls.
- Flatten each ball into a circle about ¾" thick.
- Cut each circle into 8 triangles and place on baking sheet.
- Bake for 20 minutes or until lightly browned.
- Cool scones on wire rack.
- **Make frosting:** combine powdered sugar and cinnamon, then add melted butter and milk, adding additional milk if needed (but don't add too much).
- Frost and serve!

GINGERBREAD SCONES

MAKES	PREP	READY IN
24 scones	25 minutes	50 minutes

"Better than a gingerbread man—and you don't feel bad for biting off his leg!" —Doug M., MA

INGREDIENTS

- **2½ cups** flour
- **3 tsp** baking powder
- **½ tsp** baking soda
- **⅓ cup** sugar
- **1 tsp** ground ginger
- **1 tsp** cinnamon
- **½ tsp** allspice
- **½ tsp** ground cloves
- **½ tsp** salt
- **¼ cup** dark brown sugar
- **½ cup** cold butter
- **½ cup** milk
- **1** egg
- **1 tsp** vanilla extract
- **¼ cup** molasses
- **¾–1 cup** white chocolate chips

Frosting:

- **2 oz** cream cheese, softened
- **1½ cups** powdered sugar
- **1 Tbsp** milk
- **1 tsp** vanilla extract

STEPS

- Preheat oven to 375°F. Lightly spray a cookie sheet (or line with parchment paper).
- In large bowl, combine dry ingredients.
- Cut in butter until mixture resembles coarse crumbs, then stir in chips.
- In separate bowl, mix milk, egg, vanilla, and molasses. Add to flour/butter mixture in large bowl, adding more milk if dough is too crumbly to stay together.
- Turn dough out onto floured surface and divide into three 12-oz pieces; shape into balls.
- Flatten each ball into a circle about ¾" thick.
- Cut each circle into 8 triangles and place on baking sheet.
- Bake for 20–25 minutes or until lightly browned.
- While scones cool slightly, mix the frosting ingredients.
- Frost and serve!

"The aroma of these scones baking brings out the feelings of family and holiday traditions." —Julie M., MA

ESPRESSO CHIP SCONES

MAKES
24 scones

PREP
20 minutes

READY IN
45 minutes

INGREDIENTS

Scones:

- **3 cups** flour
- **½ cup** sugar
- **5 tsp** baking powder
- **1 tsp** salt
- **1 tsp** fresh coffee grounds
- **1 cup** cold butter
- **¾–1 cup** espresso chips
- **¼ cup** milk
- **¼ cup** strong coffee
- **1 egg**

Frosting:

- **1½ cups** powdered sugar
- **1 tsp** fresh coffee grounds
- **2 Tbsp** melted butter
- **1 Tbsp** strong coffee

STEPS

- Preheat oven to 375°F.

- In large bowl, mix flour, sugar, baking powder, salt, and fresh coffee grounds.

- Cut in butter until mixture resembles coarse crumbs.

- Stir in espresso chips.

- In separate bowl, mix milk, strong coffee, and egg, then add to flour/butter mixture in large bowl.

- As you mix, add more coffee if the dough is too crumbly to stick together.

- Divide dough into 3 12-oz pieces and shape into balls.

- Flatten each ball into a circle about ¾" thick.

- Cut each circle into 8 triangles and place on baking sheet.

- Bake for 20 minutes or until lightly browned.

- Let scones cool slightly while you mix the frosting ingredients, adding additional strong coffee for desired consistency (but don't add too much). Frost and serve!

CARAMEL (OR FROSTED) CINNAMON ROLLS

MAKES

12-15 rolls

PREP

45 minutes

READY IN

3½ hours

INGREDIENTS

Dough:
- **1 Tbsp** yeast (or 1 package)
- **1¼ cups** lukewarm milk
- **¼ cup** sugar
- **1 tsp** salt
- **1** egg
- **4 Tbsp** butter, softened
- **3½–4 cups** flour

Filling:
- **3 Tbsp** butter, melted
- **½ cup** sugar
- **2½ tsp** cinnamon

Toppings:

Option 1—Frosted Rolls

Option 2—Caramel Rolls
- **½ cup** butter
- **½ cup** brown sugar, packed and mounded
- **1 Tbsp** light Karo syrup
- **1 cup** chopped nuts (walnuts, almonds, pecans, etc.)

STEPS

- In large bowl, dissolve yeast in lukewarm milk.
- Add sugar, salt, egg, and butter, and mix until smooth.
- Work flour into the mixture until dough handles easily.
- Turn out and knead dough until smooth and elastic, about 15 minutes (or knead in a KitchenAid mixer).
- Place dough in large, greased mixing bowl. Lightly spread a bit of salad oil over top of dough.
- Cover bowl with cloth; let rise in a warm place until doubled in size, about 60 minutes.
- Roll dough into an 8" x 14" rectangle, long side closest to you; dough should be ~½" thick.
- For filling: brush dough with melted butter and sprinkle with cinnamon and sugar.
- Roll up dough, starting from the long edge, stretching slightly as you go.
- Seal edge carefully and tightly, evening up the roll.

Option 1: Frosted Rolls

- Cut dough roll into ¾–1" thick slices and arrange 3 by 5 in greased 9" x 13" pan.

- Let rise 45–60 minutes.

- Preheat oven to 350°F and bake 25–30 minutes or until lightly browned.

- Cool for about 15 minutes, then frost with Cream Cheese Frosting (recipe, p. 60), but reduce powdered sugar to 1¾ **lbs** (about 7 cups).

Option 2: Caramel Rolls

- In 1-qt saucepan, combine butter, brown sugar, and Karo syrup.

- Heat and stir, almost bringing to a boil, and then immediately pour into a 9" x 13" baking pan. Sprinkle with chopped nuts.

- Cut roll of dough into ¾–1" thick slices and arrange 3 by 5 on top of caramel mixture.

- Let rise 45–60 minutes.

- Preheat oven to 350°F and bake 25–30 minutes or until lightly browned.

- After removing rolls from oven, immediately invert them onto a cookie sheet, using a spatula to scrape the topping left in the pan onto the rolls.

"These cinnamon rolls are Christmas morning and a rainy Saturday afternoon in flannel jammies in front of a warm fireplace, all wrapped into one. A mug of hot coffee is a necessary addition!" —Christi B., CA

Back in the 1960's, Sue Gregg, the food service director at a camp, originated this caramel recipe. She baked it once a week on "Hike Day," establishing a tradition honored for decades. Frosted cinnamon rolls eventually became a mainstream obsession, so the caramel version was supplanted, but our family still believes there's nothing like a hot, melty, caramelly cinnamon roll on special occasions.

Desserts

Sweetness shared

How sweet are your words to my taste,
sweeter than honey to my mouth!   —Psalm 119:103

FRESH APPLE PIE

MAKES	PREP	READY IN
1 pie	45 minutes	2 hours

Use Granny Smith or any other good baking apples. Cool for at least 30 minutes and then serve this à la mode. Delicious!

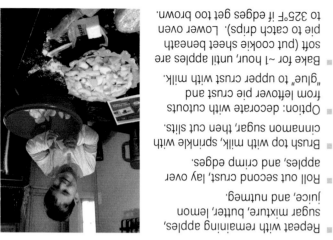

"I'm pretty sure this pie could solve a lot of the world's problems!" —Matt L., MA

INGREDIENTS

- 2 raw pie crust balls (recipe, p. 43)
- **½–¾ cup** sugar
- **2 Tbsp** cinnamon
- **2 Tbsp** flour
- **7-8 medium-large apples,** peeled and sliced
- **3 Tbsp** butter
- **2 tsp** lemon juice
- **¼ tsp** freshly grated nutmeg
- milk *(for brushing top crust)*
- cinnamon sugar *(for top crust)*

STEPS

- Preheat oven to 350°F (325°F if using a glass pie pan).
- Roll out one pie crust; lay over bottom of 9-10" pie plate.
- In separate bowl, mix sugar, cinnamon, and flour.
- Put half the apples in pie shell and sprinkle with half of the sugar mixture.
- Cut butter into pieces, then dot pie with half the pieces. Sprinkle with half the lemon juice and half the nutmeg.
- Repeat with remaining apples, sugar mixture, butter, lemon juice, and nutmeg.
- Roll out second crust, lay over apples, and crimp edges.
- Brush top with milk, sprinkle with cinnamon sugar, then cut slits.
- Option: decorate with cutouts from leftover pie crust and "glue" to upper crust with milk.
- Bake for ~1 hour, until apples are soft (put cookie sheet beneath pie to catch drips). Lower oven to 325°F if edges get too brown.

APPLE CRISP

SERVES
6–8

PREP
15 minutes

READY IN
1 hour

INGREDIENTS

7–8 medium-large apples

¼ cup flour

⅓ cup cold butter

¾ cup brown sugar, packed

1 tsp cinnamon

¼ tsp salt

1 cup oats

⅝ cup cinnamon sugar (*for sprinkling apples*)

2 Tbsp butter

STEPS

- Preheat oven to 350°F. Spray a 9" deep-dish pie pan with cooking spray—or use two 8" cake pans.

- Peel and slice apples.

- In a bowl, mix flour, butter, brown sugar, cinnamon, salt, and oats until crumbly.

- Spread apples in pan(s) and sprinkle with cinnamon sugar (we use ½ **cup** sugar mixed with **2 Tbsp** cinnamon).

- Dot with butter, then spread the crumbled oat mixture on top.

- Lower oven to 325°F if using a glass pie pan. Bake for 45 minutes or until apples are soft.

PUMPKIN PIE

MAKES	PREP	READY IN
1 9" pie	20 minutes	1½ hours

I like to "decorate" my pie with the excess pie dough. Re-roll leftover scraps and cut with cookie cutter shapes to "float" on top of the uncooked pie.

INGREDIENTS

1 pie crust (recipe, p. 43)

¾ cup sugar

2 tsp cinnamon

1 tsp ground ginger

½ tsp ground cloves

½ tsp salt

2 eggs, large

15-oz can pumpkin
(or 2 cups freshly puréed
pumpkin—recipe, p. 41)

12-oz can evaporated milk

STEPS

- Preheat oven to 425°F. Roll out pie crust and place in a 9" deep-dish pie pan.

- In a small bowl, mix together sugar, cinnamon, ginger, cloves, and salt.

- In a large bowl, beat eggs, then stir in pumpkin and evaporated milk.

- Stir sugar mixture into pumpkin mixture and pour into unbaked pie shell.

- Bake for 15 minutes, then reduce temperature to 350°F and bake 40–50 minutes longer, or until knife inserted near center comes out clean.

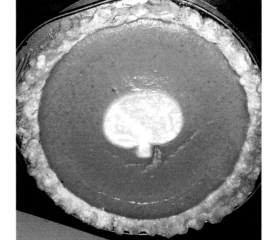

SHARE WITH THE LORD'S PEOPLE WHO ARE IN NEED.

Practice hospitality

ROMANS 12:13

ROASTED PUMPKIN SEEDS

- Preheat oven to 350°F.

- In large bowl, add the scooped-out pumpkin seeds and any attached pulp.

- Add water and whisk by hand until the seeds separate out. They should float to the top.

- Skim the seeds off and drain in colander.

- Pat dry, then toss with garlic oil and salt.

- Spread on lightly greased baking sheet, then roast for 30–40 minutes or until golden brown.

- Remove from oven. Cool on pan.

- Eat as is, or use to garnish soups and salads.

PUMPKIN PURÉE

- Preheat oven to 350°F.

- Cut a pumpkin in half*, then scoop out the seeds and stringy flesh. (Save the seeds—you can roast them and snack on them later!)

- Place the pumpkin halves face down on a baking sheet lined with foil, parchment paper, or a silicone baking mat.

- Bake until soft, about 45–60 minutes.

- Cool. Scoop out the flesh, then purée the cooked pumpkin in food processor or VitaMix-type blender. Whatever isn't used immediately, freeze in 2-cup portions in a ziplock bag for pumpkin year-round.

*If you are working with pumpkin pieces, roast (or boil) them until tender, then remove and discard the skin before mashing or blending.

STRAWBERRY CREAM PIE

MAKES
1 pie

PREP
30 minutes

READY IN
2 hours

Fresh peaches or any fresh berries may be substituted for the strawberries. This pie is best eaten all in one day, as the crust will get soggy over time.

INGREDIENTS

Filling:

1 pie crust (recipe, p. 43)

3 oz cream cheese, softened

½ cup powdered sugar

1 tsp almond extract

1 cup whipping cream, whipped (or *Cool Whip*)

1 pint fresh strawberries, cleaned and hulled

Glaze:

1 Tbsp cornstarch, heaping

¾ cup water, divided

½ cup sugar

1 Tbsp strawberry jello, unprepared

STEPS

- Prepare and bake one 9" pie crust (or use a graham cracker crust).

- **Prepare glaze:** in a saucepan over medium heat, first dissolve cornstarch in ¼ cup water to avoid lumping.

- Add sugar and remaining ¼ cup water, then cook until thickened.

- Stir in jello powder, remove from heat, and set aside to cool.

- **Prepare filling:** cream together cream cheese, powdered sugar, and extract.

- Fold in whipped cream, then spread into cooled pie crust.

- Arrange berries on cream layer.

- Pour cooled glaze over berries.

- Cover and refrigerate pie for at least 1 hour, but not more than 4 hours.

PERFECT PIE CRUST

MAKES

4 9"-pie crusts

PREP

45 minutes

READY IN

2 hours

This recipe makes 4 single crusts. Unused dough can be kept tightly wrapped in refrigerator for up to three days, or freeze. It freezes beautifully—just wrap well in Saran Wrap and stick in the freezer. Take out a few hours before you need it. Thaw in refrigerator or at room temperature. Roll while still cold.

INGREDIENTS

4 cups flour

1 Tbsp sugar

2 tsp salt

1¾ cups shortening

½ cup water

1 Tbsp vinegar (white or cider)

1 egg

STEPS

- In large bowl, mix together flour, sugar, and salt.
- Add shortening and mix until crumbly.
- In separate bowl, beat together water, vinegar, and egg.
- Add egg mixture to flour mixture, then stir until moist.
- Cover dough and chill at least 1 hour.
- Divide dough into 4 equal balls.
- Roll each ball out on a floured surface and place in pie pan.
- If baking before filling: prick surface, then bake in preheated oven at 400°F for about 15 minutes, or until golden brown.

WACKY CAKE

SERVES	PREP	READY IN
8	15 minutes	1 hour 15 minutes

This egg-less recipe was developed during World War II by the "WAACS" (Women's Army Auxiliary Corps) due to egg rationing. Hence the name "wacky"—and it's our favorite chocolate cake recipe!

INGREDIENTS

1½ cups flour
1 cup sugar
3 Tbsp baking cocoa
1 tsp baking soda
¼ tsp salt
⅓ cup oil
1 cup water
1 Tbsp vinegar
1 tsp vanilla extract

STEPS

- Preheat oven to 350°F. Spray an 8" x 8" pan.
- Mix together flour, sugar, cocoa, baking soda, and salt.
- Add oil, water, vinegar, and vanilla and mix well.
- Pour into pan and bake for 30 minutes, or until done.
- Cool.
- Frost with Buttercream Frosting (recipe, p. 61) or Soft White Icing (recipe, p. 61).

PUMPKIN LAYER CAKE

SERVES
12

PREP
30 minutes

READY IN
1 ¾ hours

"This is a delicious pumpkin-y alternative to pie!"
—Michelle M., Foxboro

INGREDIENTS

Crust (layer 1):
1 white or yellow 2-layer cake mix, divided
½ cup butter, melted
1 egg

Filling (layer 2):
1 lb pumpkin purée (recipe, p. 41)
3 eggs
1¼ cups evaporated milk
½ cup sugar
1 tsp cinnamon

½ tsp ground ginger
¼ tsp ground cloves
¼ tsp salt

Topping (layer 3):
reserved cake mix
⅓ cup sugar
¼ cup cold butter
1 tsp cinnamon
½ cup chopped walnuts (optional)

STEPS

- Preheat oven to 350°F. Spray a 9" x 13" pan.
- Crust: Reserve **1 cup** of dry cake mix (for topping).
- Mix melted butter with 1 egg and the remaining dry cake mix.
- Press mixture into bottom of pan.
- Filling: Mix together pumpkin, 3 eggs, milk, sugar, cinnamon, ginger, cloves, and salt.
- Pour this pumpkin mixture into the prepared pan, over the first layer.
- Topping: Mix together the reserved dry cake mix, sugar, butter, cinnamon, and walnuts (optional).
- Sprinkle topping on pumpkin layer.
- Bake for 55–60 minutes.
- Cool. (It will set during this time.)
- Serve with whipped cream. Refrigerate any leftovers.

ALMOND PUFF PASTRY

SERVES	PREP	READY IN
6-8	40 minutes	2 hours

For Christmas, I shape the dough into a wreath, as pictured; for Easter, I shape it into a cross.

INGREDIENTS

Base:
½ **cup** butter
1 **cup** flour
2 **Tbsp** water

Filling:
½ **cup** butter
1 **cup** water
1 **tsp** almond extract
1 **cup** flour
3 eggs

Frosting:
1½ **cups** powdered sugar
2 **Tbsp** butter, melted
1½ **tsp** almond extract

Garnish:
½ **cup** toasted sliced almonds

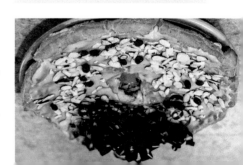

STEPS

- Preheat oven to 350°F.
- **Prepare base:** Cut butter into flour.
- Sprinkle water over flour mixture; mix with fork.
- Gather pastry into a ball, then divide in half.
- Press each piece of dough onto an ungreased cookie sheet, forming each into a 3" by 10" rectangle (or for Christmas, shape all the dough into a wreath; for Easter, a cross).
- **Prepare filling:** Heat butter and water on stove to a rolling boil; remove from heat.
- Quickly stir in almond extract and flour.
- Return to heat (low) and stir vigorously until mixture forms a ball, about one minute. Remove from heat.
- Add eggs; beat until smooth and glossy.
- Spread mixture (divided evenly) over both rectangles.
- Bake for 1 hour. The filling will be crisp and brown.
- Cool. Filling will shrink and fall, forming a custardy top.
- **Prepare frosting:** Mix powdered sugar, butter, and almond extract, using a small amount of warm water as needed to bring to desired consistency.
- Frost cooled pastry. When frosting is set, sprinkle with sliced almonds.

FRUIT PIZZA

MAKES
2 12" pizzas

PREP
45 minutes

READY IN
4 hours

"Fruit pizza has always been my birthday dessert of choice!" —Lisa F., CA

INGREDIENTS

Cookie base:
1 cup butter
1½ cups powdered sugar
1 egg
1 tsp vanilla extract
½ tsp almond extract
2½ cups flour
1 tsp baking soda
1 tsp cream of tartar

Cream cheese spread:
16 oz cream cheese
1 cup sugar
2 tsp almond extract

Fruit:
sliced kiwi, blueberries, sliced peaches, sliced strawberries, raspberries, blackberries, etc.

Glaze:
1 cup sugar
1 cup orange juice
¼ cup lemon juice
¾ cup water
2 Tbsp cornstarch
¼ tsp salt

STEPS

- Cream butter and sugar.
- Add egg and extracts; mix thoroughly.
- Sift together flour, baking soda, and cream of tartar and blend in.
- Refrigerate 2 to 3 hours.
- Preheat oven to 375°F.
- For each 12" base, press half the dough into a greased 12" pizza pan.
- Bake 10–12 minutes or until brown around the edges. Cool.
- Blend cream cheese spread ingredients and spread half on each cookie base.
- Place fruit on top in circles.
- In saucepan, mix glaze ingredients and cook until thickened. Cool.
- Pour barely warm glaze over fruit pizzas and enjoy!

Note: You can instead make 24 to 36 "personal size" pizzas. Roll dough ³⁄₁₆" thick on a lightly floured surface. Cut with 3" round cookie cutter.

LEMONY SNAP COOKIES

READY IN 1 hour

PREP 30 minutes

MAKES 3 dozen 3" cookies

INGREDIENTS

- **2½ cups** flour
- **1½ cups** sugar
- **2 tsp** baking soda
- **¼ tsp** salt
- **2 tsp** lemon zest
- **¾ cup** vegetable oil
- **½ cup** fresh lemon juice
- **2 tsp** vanilla extract

Glaze:
- **1½ cups** powdered sugar
- **2-3 Tbsp** lemon juice

STEPS

- Preheat oven to 350°F. Lightly spray cookie sheets.
- In large mixing bowl, stir together flour, sugar, baking soda, salt, and lemon zest.
- Make a well in the center of the flour mixture and fill it with oil, lemon juice, and vanilla. Mix everything well.
- Using a #30 cookie scoop (about 1½ Tbsp of dough), make balls and place about 2" apart on cookie sheets.
- Bake for 12-14 minutes, until edges are golden brown.
- Cool on cooling rack.
- **Prepare glaze:** mix powdered sugar and lemon juice until smooth and slightly runny (but not too runny).
- Put glaze in decorator bag and pipe onto cookies (as pictured).
- Store cookies in tightly closed container (or freeze) until you're ready to serve them.

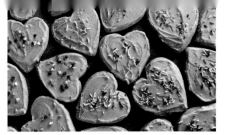

"Look no further for your 'go to' sugar cookie. Heaven in every bite!"
—Mallory H., MA

GIGI'S SUGAR COOKIES

MAKES
3 dozen 3" cookies

PREP
15 minutes

READY IN
4 hours

INGREDIENTS

Cookies:

1½ cups sifted powdered sugar

1 cup butter, softened

1 egg

2 tsp almond extract

2½ cups flour

1 tsp baking soda

1 tsp cream of tartar

Cream Cheese Frosting:
See recipe, p. 60, but replace both extracts with **2 tsp** almond extract.

STEPS

- Beat sugar and butter together.
- Add egg and extract; mix well.
- Sift together flour, baking soda, and cream of tartar, and blend into butter mixture.
- Refrigerate 2–3 hours.
- Preheat oven to 375°F.
- Roll dough on lightly floured surface to ³⁄₁₆" thickness.
- Cut with a 3" round cookie cutter (or other shapes).
- Place on lightly greased baking sheet.
- Bake 10–12 minutes or until delicately golden.
- Let cookies cool completely. Frost and serve!

"Gigi's cookies are our favorite cookies to make and eat."
—Brandon, Ana, and Micah G., CA
Nathan and Rachel J., VA

ABOUT PAUL'S CHOCOLATE CHIP COOKIES

This recipe was first shared with us by our dear friend Helen Challener. Virginia taught Paul to make them—and the rest is history. Soon they became Paul's "signature item."

On a family mission trip to Haiti in 1999, soon after the early morning flight had reached flying altitude, Paul got up and, to the delight of the children and horror of the moms, started passing out his cookies to everyone on the team. The moms said, "Paul, you can't give cookies to the kids, it's 8 am!" to which Paul responded, "Oh, it's okay, they're 'Breakfast Biscuits.'"

Over the years, Paul's chocolate chip cookies have been served at countless social gatherings, after every sporting event the Friesen girls were ever in, during check-in at H.I.M. Marriage Conferences, and, for 22 years, to the New England Patriots couples during our in-season couples' Bible studies.

We've found the yield can vary. A single recipe has made 24-28 cookies, depending on whether or not Paul is "off sugar."

The Haiti Mission Team that first ate "breakfast biscuits"—launching a whole new terminology.

Special Tips:

- *Paul uses a #30 cookie scoop (about 2 Tbsp) for uniform cookies.*
- *He also likes to use AirBake® pans so the bottoms do not overbake.*
- *If you are not consuming the cookies on the day they are baked, we suggest freezing them in a ziplock bag.*
- *You can also form the dough into balls and "quick freeze" them: scoop the dough onto a cookie sheet just as you would if you were planning to bake them immediately, but freeze the frozen dough balls instead. Then transfer the frozen dough balls into a ziplock bag. When you need a cookie (or three!) just bake straight from their frozen state. Frozen dough may need a minute or two longer in the oven.*

PAUL'S CHOCOLATE CHIP COOKIES

SERVES

1 teenager

PREP

20 minutes

READY IN

30 minutes

INGREDIENTS

1 egg

¾ cup white granulated sugar

¾ cup light brown sugar, firmly packed

1 cup butter, softened

2 ½ cups flour

1 tsp baking soda

½ tsp salt

6-12 oz chocolate chips

The secret to soft cookies is to cook by faith, not by sight.

STEPS

- Preheat oven to 375°F.
- Mix together egg, white sugar, brown sugar, and butter.
- In separate bowl, mix flour, baking soda, and salt.
- Add flour mixture into butter mixture.
- Mix in chocolate chips.
- Drop by 1–1½ Tablespoonfuls (use a cookie scoop if possible: #40 or #30 scoop) onto ungreased cookie sheets—AirBake pans are the best, if available.
- Bake for 10 minutes or until edges are brown.

ROSEMARY GINGERSNAPS

MAKES	PREP	READY IN
3 dozen cookies	25 minutes	40 minutes

INGREDIENTS

- **¾ cup** butter
- **1 cup** sugar
- 1 egg
- **¼ cup** molasses
- **2 cups** whole wheat flour
- **1 tsp** baking soda
- **1 tsp** salt
- **2 tsp** dried, crumbled rosemary
- **1 tsp** ground ginger
- **½ tsp** ground cloves

For rolling:

½–1 cup raw sugar

STEPS

- Preheat oven to 350°F and lightly spray cookie sheets.
- Cream butter, then add sugar and beat until light.
- Add egg and then molasses; continue beating until mixture is fluffy.
- In separate bowl, combine dry ingredients and spices.
- Add flour mixture to butter mixture and blend.
- Scoop with #40 cookie scoop (or form into 1½" balls) and roll in raw sugar.
- Place 2" apart on cookie sheet.
- Bake for 10–12 minutes.
- Cookies will look slightly underdone, but will be light brown on bottoms.
- Let cookies cool.

"The rosemary twists this ginger cookie in a uniquely delicious direction!" —Danielle B., TX

PEANUT BUTTER CUP COOKIES

MAKES
4 dozen cookies

PREP
25 minutes

READY IN
1 hour

INGREDIENTS

1 ¾ cups flour

½ tsp salt

1 tsp baking soda

½ cup butter, softened

½ cup sugar

½ cup brown sugar, packed

½ cup peanut butter

1 egg, beaten

1 tsp vanilla extract

2 Tbsp milk

additional sugar (*for rolling*)

48 miniature peanut butter cups, unwrapped

STEPS

- Preheat oven to 375°F. Spray mini muffin pans or fill with mini paper liners.

- Sift together flour, salt, and baking soda; set aside.

- In large bowl, cream together butter, sugar, brown sugar, and peanut butter.

- Beat in egg, vanilla, and milk.

- Add flour mixture; mix well.

- Shape dough into 48 1" balls. Lightly roll in granulated sugar and place each into mini muffin pan.

These cookies use miniature peanut butter cups, which I buy on sale after every holiday and freeze so I'm ready to make them anytime. Who can resist the marriage of peanut butter and chocolate?

- Bake 8–10 minutes.

- Remove from oven and immediately place a mini peanut butter cup into the center of each ball.

- Return to oven for 4–5 minutes.

- Cool, then carefully remove from pan.

CHOCOLATE PEANUT BUTTER CHIP COOKIES

MAKES
4 dozen cookies

PREP
25 min

READY IN
40 minutes

INGREDIENTS

- **1 cup** butter, softened
- **1½ cups** sugar
- **2** eggs
- **2 tsp** vanilla extract
- **2½ cups** flour
- **⅔ cup** baking cocoa
- **1 tsp** baking soda
- **½ tsp** salt
- **2 cups** peanut butter chips (or white chocolate chips, or mint chips)

STEPS

- Preheat oven to 350°F.
- Cream butter, sugar, eggs, and vanilla until fluffy.
- In separate bowl, combine flour, cocoa, baking soda, and salt.
- Add dry ingredients to butter mixture and blend.
- Fold in chips.
- Scoop with #40 cookie scoop (or form into 1½" balls) and place on ungreased baking sheet.
- Bake for 10-12 minutes or until they're set.
- Cookies will look slightly underdone, but they'll be ready.
- Let cool on cookie sheet for 5-10 minutes before removing to a wire rack to continue cooling.

PISTACHIO-CRANBERRY BISCOTTI

MAKES
30 cookies

PREP
30 min

READY IN
1½ hours

This recipe hits the right combination of chewiness: not too hard, not too soft, just right—and the flavor is out of this world.

INGREDIENTS

1¾ cups flour
1 tsp baking powder
½ tsp salt
¼ cup butter, softened
¾ cup sugar
2 tsp vanilla extract
1 tsp almond extract
2 eggs
2 cups chopped unsalted pistachios (or slivered almonds)
¾ cup dried cranberries (or dried cherries), coarsely chopped

STEPS

- Preheat oven to 350°F. Line a cookie sheet with parchment paper.
- Sift together flour, baking powder, and salt; set aside.
- In large bowl, cream together the butter, sugar, and extracts.
- Beat in eggs. Fold in nuts and cranberries.
- Add flour mixture and mix on low speed until well combined.
- Turn dough out onto floured surface and, with floured hands, divide into two pieces, gently shaping each piece into a "log" about 2" wide and 12" long.
- Place "logs" onto cookie sheet about 3" apart.
- Bake for 20–25 minutes until golden brown and firm to the touch.
- Let cool for 10 minutes before carefully removing logs (one at a time) to a cutting board.
- With a serrated knife, slice each log diagonally into ¾"-thick pieces.
- Lower oven temperature to 300°F.
- Place each slice of biscotti on the same cookie sheet, cut sides down, and bake 10 minutes.
- Turn each slice over, then bake an additional 10 minutes.
- Let cool on wire racks. Store in airtight container.

OATMEAL RAISIN COOKIES

MAKES	PREP	READY IN
3 dozen	15 min	35 minutes

"The perfect oatmeal-raisin cookie, without a doubt!"
—David L., VA

INGREDIENTS

1 **cup** butter, softened

1⅓ **cups** brown sugar, packed

2 eggs

1 **tsp** vanilla extract

1½ **cups** flour

1 **tsp** baking soda

2 **tsp** cinnamon

1 **tsp** salt

3 **cups** rolled oats

1½ **cups** raisins

STEPS

- Preheat oven to 350°F. Spray cookie sheets with cooking spray.
- Cream the butter and brown sugar.
- Add eggs and vanilla; mix thoroughly.
- In separate bowl, combine flour, baking soda, cinnamon, salt, and oats.
- Mix the wet and dry ingredients together, then stir in raisins.
- Scoop dough with #30 cookie scoop (or form into 1½" balls) and place 2" apart on cookie sheet.
- Bake for 12–14 minutes, or until golden brown around edges. Don't overbake!
- Let cookies cool on the baking sheet for 5 minutes before removing to cooling racks.

CRISPY OATMEAL COCONUT COOKIES

MAKES
3½ dozen

PREP
15 min

READY IN
30 minutes

INGREDIENTS

1½ cups butter, softened

1½ cups sugar

¾ cup brown sugar, packed

2 eggs

2 tsp vanilla extract

1¾ cups flour

2¼ cups rolled oats

1¼ cups flaked coconut

1½ tsp baking soda

1½ tsp baking powder

STEPS

- Preheat oven to 350°F.

- Cream the butter and both sugars.

- Add eggs and vanilla; mix thoroughly.

- In separate bowl, combine flour, oats, coconut, baking soda, and baking powder.

- Mix the wet and dry ingredients together.

- Scoop dough with #30 cookie scoop (or shape into 1½" balls) and place 2" apart on ungreased cookie sheets.

- Bake for 10–12 minutes, or until golden brown around edges. The middles should look slightly underbaked.

"This cookie is the perfect combination of easy-to-make and great taste. I've made them several times in a single week; we never seem to have enough!"
—Seth H., CA

PEANUT BUTTER SWIRL BARS

MAKES	PREP	READY IN
24 bars	15 minutes	1 hour

INGREDIENTS

½ cup peanut butter

⅓ cup butter

⅝ cup sugar

¾ cup brown sugar

2 eggs

2 tsp vanilla extract

1 cup flour

1 tsp baking powder

¼ tsp salt

1 cup chocolate chips

STEPS

- Preheat oven to 350°F. Spray a 9" x 13" pan.
- Cream the peanut butter, butter, and sugars.
- Beat in eggs and vanilla extract.
- Sift together and stir in the flour, baking powder, and salt.
- Spread batter in pan, then sprinkle lightly with chocolate chips.
- Bake for 5 minutes, then remove and swirl in chocolate chips.
- Return to oven for 25 minutes. Do not overbake!
- Cool, then cut into 24 bars.

"Everyone loves peanut butter and chocolate together—and a bar is quicker than cookies!"
—Laura L., VA

CARAMEL CORN

MAKES
3 quarts

PREP
30 minutes

READY IN
1½ hours

It's best not to make this on a rainy, humid day as the baked caramel corn will become sticky. This can be doubled by doubling all ingredients and baking in a turkey roaster or other large pan. Temperature and times all remain the same.

"I've been known to ask my husband to hide this from me. Can't. Stop. Eating. It."
—Barbara S., MA

INGREDIENTS

10 cups warm popped popcorn

1½ cups cocktail peanuts (*optional*)

½ cup butter

1 cup light brown sugar, packed

¼ cup light Karo syrup

¼ tsp salt

½ tsp baking powder

½ tsp vanilla extract (*or butter flavoring*)

STEPS

- Preheat oven to 250°F.

- Combine popcorn and (optionally) nuts in a 9" x 13" pan and place in oven while making the caramel syrup.

- In heavy 2-qt saucepan, melt butter.

- Stir in sugar, Karo syrup, and salt.

- Bring to a rolling boil, stirring constantly.

- Over medium heat, continue to boil **without stirring** for 5 minutes.

- Remove from heat, then add baking powder and vanilla, stirring vigorously until syrup is a light caramel color.

- Remove pan of popcorn from oven and quickly pour syrup over top, tossing until kernels and nuts are well coated.

- Return pan to oven and bake for 25 minutes, then stir well. Bake for an additional 20 minutes.

- Remove from oven and spread out on aluminum foil to cool.

- Break into pieces and store in tightly covered container.

MOCHA CHOCOLATE FROSTING

FROSTS 1 cake **PREP** 15 minutes **READY IN** 15 minutes

INGREDIENTS

5 Tbsp butter
2 Tbsp baking cocoa
1 tsp instant coffee, mixed with 1 tsp hot water to dissolve (or use espresso or very strong coffee)
1/4 tsp salt
1 tsp vanilla extract
2½ cups powdered sugar
1 Tbsp sour cream
2+ Tbsp half-and-half

STEPS

- Melt butter in 1-qt saucepan over medium heat.
- Add cocoa, instant coffee, salt, and vanilla, stirring well with wire whisk.
- Transfer to mixer bowl and beat in sugar.
- Add sour cream and 2 Tbsp half-and-half, slowly adding more half-and-half until frosting is smooth and spreadable.

CREAM CHEESE FROSTING

FROSTS 1 cake **PREP** 10 minutes **READY IN** 10 minutes

INGREDIENTS

½ cup butter, softened
8 oz cream cheese, softened
1 tsp vanilla extract
1 tsp almond extract
2 lb powdered sugar
milk to thin, if needed

STEPS

- Cream together the butter, cream cheese, and extracts.
- Add sugar, then dribble in milk to reach desired consistency.

This makes lots of frosting, which will keep well in the freezer or refrigerator.

"The frosting is so good that you don't even need the cookie—just a spoon will do!" —Kirsten W, GA

SOFT WHITE ICING

FROSTS
1 cake

PREP
10 minutes

READY IN
10 minutes

This recipe, sourced from Joyce Friesen Rottschafer, is a favorite. Less sweet but soft and fluffy, it is a crowd-pleaser, especially on Wacky Cake. Frosts one 9" x 13" cake or a 9" layer cake. Refrigeration is fine, but not necessary.

INGREDIENTS

¼ cup flour

1 cup milk

½ cup butter

½ cup shortening

1 cup sugar

1 tsp vanilla extract

STEPS

- In small saucepan, cook and stir flour and milk together over medium heat. Cool.

- Beat butter, shortening, and sugar together until fluffy.

- Add milk mixture to butter mixture, along with vanilla. Beat together.

BUTTERCREAM FROSTING

FROSTS
1 cake

PREP
5 minutes

READY IN
5 minutes

The flavor of this frosting may be varied by substituting fruit juice for the milk, adding grated orange or lemon rind, or substituting another extract for the vanilla.

This can be made early in the day, omitting the milk, and left at room temperature. Milk can then be added just before frosting cake for a smooth, easy-to-apply frosting.

INGREDIENTS

⅜ cup butter

2 cups powdered sugar

2 tsp vanilla extract

milk, to desired consistency

STEPS

- Cream together the butter, sugar, and vanilla.

- Add milk to reach desired consistency.

Vegetables and Salads

Fresh and Refresh

Better a small serving of vegetables with love
than a fattened calf with hatred.   —Proverbs 15:17

GRILL SIDE SALAD

A summertime favorite! Make it a complete meal by topping with cooked and chilled chicken or steak.
Left over, it adds zest to a hamburger, or makes a perfect filling for an omelette or a dip for tortilla chips.

SERVES
4–6

PREP
20 min

READY IN
4 hours

INGREDIENTS

- **2** medium tomatoes, chopped (about 2 cups)
- **1** medium zucchini, diced
- **1 cup** frozen whole kernel corn, thawed *(or use fresh)*
- **⅓ cup** thinly sliced green onions, with tops
- **1** small ripe avocado, coarsely chopped
- **⅓ cup** Picante sauce
- **2 Tbsp** vegetable oil
- **2 Tbsp** chopped fresh cilantro or parsley
- **1 Tbsp** lemon or lime juice
- **¾ tsp** garlic salt
- **¼ tsp** ground cumin

STEPS

- Combine tomatoes, corn, zucchini, green onions, and avocado in bowl.
- In separate bowl, whisk together remaining ingredients.
- Pour over vegetable mixture; mix gently.
- Chill for 3–4 hours, occasionally stirring gently.
- Stir and serve chilled (or at room temperature) with additional Picante sauce.
- Makes about 4 cups.

BRUSCHETTA

SERVES
4-6

PREP
15 minutes

READY IN
15 minutes

This "summer on a toast" is a delicious appetizer or side dish.

INGREDIENTS

1 lb fresh ripe tomatoes, chopped

2 cloves garlic, minced (about 2 tsp)

8 fresh basil leaves, chopped

1 Tbsp olive oil

2 tsp balsamic vinegar

1/2 tsp salt

1/2 tsp black pepper (coarse or freshly ground)

1 baguette or French bread

1/4 cup olive oil

STEPS

- In bowl, gently mix tomatoes, garlic, and basil leaves.
- In small bowl, whisk olive oil, balsamic vinegar, salt, and pepper. Stir into tomato mixture.
- This topping can be made for immediate use, or stored (covered) for several hours in the refrigerator before using.
- Slice baguette in 1/4" slices and brush each lightly with olive oil.
- Just before serving, toast or grill the slices.
- Top toast slices with tomato mixture and serve!

SHRIMP AND AVOCADO SALAD

SERVES	PREP	READY IN
2	20 min	3 hours

INGREDIENTS

- **½ lb** cooked, tail-off, deveined shrimp, cut into bite-sized pieces
- **½ cup** diced celery
- **1 Tbsp** finely diced onion
- **1 Tbsp** mayonnaise
- pepper to taste
- 1 fresh, ripe avocado
- lettuce (for serving)

"Gluten-free, healthy, filling, and—best of all—it's avocado bliss!" —Barbara S, MA

STEPS

- In medium bowl, combine shrimp, celery, onion, mayonnaise, and pepper.
- Chill for several hours prior to serving so the flavors can blend.
- Just before serving, cut avocado in half, remove pit, and carefully scoop out flesh as two whole pieces.
- Place each avocado half on a bed of lettuce.
- Scoop half of the shrimp salad onto each avocado "boat."
- Serve and go to culinary heaven.

WILD RICE AND CHICKEN SALAD

SERVES
4-6

PREP
30 min

READY IN
3 ½ hours + overnight

INGREDIENTS

4 boneless chicken breasts

¾ cup soy sauce (*for marinating*)

4 cups cooked wild rice

3-4 Tbsp vegetable oil

2 Tbsp grated fresh ginger

2 Tbsp grated fresh garlic

1 cup diced celery

1 small red onion, finely diced

½ cup mayonnaise

2 cups cut grapes

½ cup toasted sliced almonds

STEPS

▪ Cut chicken breasts into bite-size chunks and marinate in soy sauce for 2-3 hours in the refrigerator.

▪ Cook wild rice to yield 4 cups (1 cup uncooked rice yields 3 cups cooked).

▪ Heat oil in frying pan or wok and stir-fry chicken chunks along with the ginger and garlic. (We use a microplaner to grate these.)

▪ In a bowl, combine the cooked rice and the cooked chicken.

▪ Stir in celery, onion, and mayonnaise (use less or more mayonnaise, to taste).

▪ Cover bowl and chill overnight.

▪ Just before serving, stir in grapes.

▪ You may stir in the almonds as well, or, if you prefer, serve them in a dish on the side and let people add them (that way, if there's salad left over, you won't have soggy almonds).

"An irresistible hearty salad full of flavor, texture, and color—the perfect pairing of sweet and savory." —Helen C., NY

CHOPPED SALAD

SERVES	PREP	READY IN
4-6	30 minutes	30 minutes

"Add a grilled meat and you have a complete, healthy meal." —Laura L., VA

INGREDIENTS

3 cups chopped crunchy vegetables (we use radishes, zucchini, green beans, carrots, and broccoli, but also consider cucumbers, peppers, or corn)

2 cups thinly sliced lettuce (we use iceberg, but consider romaine, red leaf, or Boston)

½ cup (2 oz) crumbled feta cheese (or queso fresco)

2 green onions, thinly sliced

1-2 Tbsp thinly sliced mint leaves

½-1 cup sunflower seeds, salted (optional)

Dressing:

4 Tbsp fresh lime juice

4 Tbsp olive oil

½ tsp coarse salt

¼ tsp chili powder

¼ tsp ground cumin

freshly ground black pepper, to taste

STEPS

- In medium bowl, mix vegetables, lettuce, crumbled cheese, green onions, and mint.
- In separate bowl, whisk together all dressing ingredients.
- Pour dressing over vegetables, tossing to coat evenly.
- Adjust with more salt or pepper as needed.
- Garnish with more mint, if desired.
- Serve with a dish of sunflower seeds on the side, if desired.

FRESH VEGGIE PIZZA

SERVES
6 as main dish,
10 as appetizer

PREP
25 minutes

READY IN
3 hours

INGREDIENTS

8-oz can crescent roll dough (*or refrigerated pizza dough*)

2½ cups diced fresh vegetables (*we use radishes, broccoli florets, zucchini, green beans, carrots, cauliflower, mushrooms, and sweet peppers*)

8 oz cream cheese (*can be low-fat*)

½ cup mayonnaise (*can be low-fat*)

½ packet dry ranch dressing mix

⅓ cup shredded cheddar cheese (*or Mexican blend*)

This makes a great appetizer when cut into 1" x 2" rectangles—or it can be a meatless main dish.

STEPS

- Preheat oven to 350°F.

- Press dough out (~¼" thick) onto lightly greased 10" x 15" rimmed baking sheet and bake for 10 minutes.

- While the crust is cooling, chop the vegetables.

- In a bowl, blend the cream cheese, mayonnaise, and ranch dressing mix.

- Spread cream cheese mixture onto cooled crust.

- Top with chopped vegetables.

- Sprinkle with shredded cheese.

- Refrigerate for several hours prior to serving.

CAPRESE SALAD

The quintessential summer highlight: fresh tomatoes, fresh basil, and fresh mozzarella team up for this hard-to-beat combination, both pleasing to the eye and to the stomach.

SERVES	PREP	READY IN
Your choice!	10 minutes	10 minutes

INGREDIENTS

in-season tomatoes, sliced (use beefsteak, heirloom, or other fleshy tomatoes)

fresh mozzarella cheese, sliced

fresh basil

olive oil

balsamic vinegar

flake salt

STEPS

- On a rimmed serving platter, layer tomato slices, mozzarella, and fresh basil.
- Drizzle with olive oil and balsamic vinegar.
- Season with flake salt and serve immediately.

This recipe, from our son-in-law Derek, is a summer winner. There are no amounts listed—simply prepare the number of tomato slices you need for your "eaters" and then repeat with the fresh mozzarella, one slice per tomato slice. Apply the remaining ingredients in quantities to your liking.

ROASTED BEET SALAD

SERVES
4

PREP
30 minutes

READY IN
4 hours

Though beets aren't everyone's favorite, this recipe may close the gap for some. It's a delicious twist on a beautiful vegetable.

INGREDIENTS

½ lb beets

2 Tbsp olive oil, divided

salt to taste

2 Tbsp balsamic vinegar

½ cup feta cheese

½ cup toasted, coarsely chopped walnuts

lettuce (*for serving*)

STEPS

- Preheat oven to 400°F.

- Toss beets with **1 Tbsp** olive oil in a baking dish and season with salt. Pour in enough water to barely cover bottom of dish.

- Cover tightly with foil and roast for 60–75 minutes.

- Let cool, then peel off skins. Chop beets into bite-size pieces.

- Marinate for a few hours in balsamic vinegar and remaining **1 Tbsp** olive oil.

- Mix beets with feta cheese and walnuts.

- Serve on a bed of lettuce and sprinkle with extra feta cheese as a garnish.

BRUSSELS SPROUTS WITH WALNUTS AND BACON

SERVES	PREP	READY IN
4	30 minutes	1 hour

INGREDIENTS

1 lb fresh brussels sprouts, trimmed and halved

6 slices bacon, uncooked, cut into bite-size pieces

3 cloves garlic, minced

salt and pepper

¼ cup olive oil

½ cup coarsely chopped walnuts

Glaze:

¼ cup balsamic vinegar

¼ cup honey

1 Tbsp chopped fresh rosemary

STEPS

- Adjust oven rack to middle of oven and preheat oven to 425°F.

- On a large baking sheet, season brussels sprouts, bacon, and garlic with salt and pepper.

- Drizzle with oil and toss until combined.

- Bake for 15 minutes, then remove pan and stir in walnuts. Return to oven for another 15 minutes until sprouts are tender and slightly charred (about 30 minutes total).

- While sprouts are baking, make the glaze: in small saucepan, combine vinegar, honey, and rosemary.

- Simmer until reduced by half, stirring occasionally, for about 15 minutes. The mixture should coat the back of a spoon when reduced.

- Transfer roasted brussels sprouts mixture to serving dish and drizzle glaze over all.

"No better way to eat veggies than smothered in bacon and topped with walnuts. A favorite on our Thanksgiving table." —Kari G., CA

OVEN-ROASTED BROCCOLI

SERVES
4

PREP
10 minutes

READY IN
15 minutes

INGREDIENTS

1 lb broccoli

1 Tbsp olive oil

salt and pepper to taste

STEPS

- Wash broccoli and cut into florets.
- Spread on baking sheet; drizzle with oil and sprinkle with salt and pepper.
- Adjust oven racks so that pan will be 6"–8" from broiler coils, then set oven to high broil.
- Broil for 2 minutes, stir, then broil for 2 minutes more.

SPINACH BROCCOLI CASSEROLE

SERVES
10

PREP
10 minutes

READY IN
30 minutes

INGREDIENTS

2 10-oz boxes frozen chopped broccoli

3 10-oz boxes frozen chopped spinach

1 pint sour cream

1 envelope Lipton dry onion soup mix

1 cup grated cheddar cheese

STEPS

- Preheat oven to 350°F. Spray a 9" x 13" pan.
- Cook broccoli and spinach according to package directions until almost tender, then drain and combine.
- Mix in sour cream and soup mix.
- Pour into prepared pan and top with grated cheese.
- Bake for 20 minutes or until cheese is melted.

SWEET POTATO FRIES

SERVES
4

PREP
20 minutes

READY IN
1¾ hours

These oven-roasted (not fried!) sweet potato fries are a satisfying and healthy side dish.

INGREDIENTS

- **3** medium sweet potatoes
- **2 Tbsp** cornstarch
- **2 Tbs** olive oil
- **1 tsp** garlic powder
- **1 tsp** paprika
- **1 tsp** salt
- **½ tsp** black pepper

STEPS

- Wash sweet potatoes and cut into ¼" sticks (leave skin on).
- Soak sticks in cold water for 1 hour.
- Dry sticks completely with towel (or air-dry if you have time).
- Preheat oven to 400°F.
- In a bag, toss sticks with cornstarch and shake until well coated.
- In a bowl, mix oil and spices.
- Add sticks to oil, toss well, then spread in single layer on rimmed baking sheet.
- Bake about 15 minutes, until brown and crisp on the bottom, then flip and bake until other side is crisp, about 10 minutes.
- For extra-crispy fries, broil for the last 5 minutes, watching carefully so as not to burn them.

WHEN YOU EAT AND ARE SATISFIED,
BE CAREFUL THAT YOU

do not forget the Lord

DEUTERONOMY 6:11–12

SWEET POTATO CASSEROLE

SERVES
6-8

PREP
20 minutes

READY IN
1 ¼ hours

INGREDIENTS

2 lbs fresh sweet potatoes or yams, peeled, chunked, and boiled until soft (*or use puréed pumpkin*)

¼ cup butter

¼ cup brown sugar

1 egg

1 tsp vanilla extract

Topping:

¼ cup cold butter

½ cup brown sugar

1 tsp vanilla extract

½ cup chopped pecans

This makes a great side dish at Thanksgiving or for a Christmas turkey or ham.

STEPS

- Preheat oven to 350°F.
- In bowl, whip together cooked yams, butter, brown sugar, egg, and vanilla.
- Pour into oven-proof casserole dish.
- Mix topping ingredients together until crumbly and sprinkle evenly over potatoes.
- Bake for about 45 minutes, or until top is bubbly.

Main Dishes
An Open Door

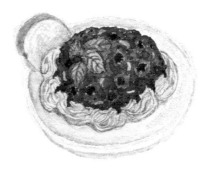

"For I was hungry and you gave me something to eat,
I was thirsty and you gave me something to drink,
I was a stranger and you invited me in" — Matthew 25:35

FRITTATA

SERVES
6-8

PREP
15 minutes

READY IN
40 minutes

"Uncle Paul's frittata is pure delight in every bite!"
—Rachael C., CA

INGREDIENTS

1 Tbsp olive oil
1 medium onion, diced
3 cloves garlic, minced
4 oz mushrooms, sliced
1 lb fresh spinach
6 oz uncooked bacon, cut into ½" pieces
6 eggs
½ cup feta cheese
½ tsp pepper
1 tomato, diced
¼ cup shredded cheese

STEPS

- Preheat oven to 350°F. Spray a 9"x13" pan or 10" round casserole with cooking spray.
- Heat oil in frying pan, then over medium heat, sauté onion, mushrooms, and garlic.
- Add spinach slowly to pan (or sauté in separate pan).
- Transfer sautéed vegetables to large mixing bowl.
- Fry bacon, then drain and add to bowl.
- In separate bowl, beat eggs, then add to vegetables along with the feta cheese.
- Add salt and pepper. Stir.
- Pour mixture into prepared pan.
- Bake for 20 minutes or until firm.
- Remove from oven and top with diced tomato and shredded cheese.
- Return to oven just long enough to melt the cheese.

Optional toppings: avocado slices, salsa

Substitutions: other cheeses, breakfast meats, and vegetables can be substituted (or left out) as desired.

BEEF OLÉ

SERVES
8

PREP
30 minutes

READY IN
1 ½ hours

This is a great meal to serve a crowd because each person builds their own creation using the ingredients of their choice.

INGREDIENTS

Meat sauce:

2 lbs ground beef (*or turkey*)

1 onion, chopped

28 oz tomato sauce

2 ¼ tsp chili powder (*or to taste*)

⅛ tsp cumin

¾ tsp garlic powder

1 ½ tsp salt

¾ tsp pepper

pinch oregano

4-oz can green chilis, chopped

Serve with the following in separate bowls:

1 bag tortilla chips

½ lb shredded cheese

½ head lettuce, shredded

2 fresh tomatoes, chopped

Toppings:

salsa
chopped olives
bean sprouts
refried beans
sliced avocados (*or guacamole*)
sour cream

STEPS

- In Dutch oven, brown meat and onions; pour off fat.
- Stir in tomato sauce, spices, and chilis.
- Simmer over low heat for at least one hour.
- Serve buffet-style with a choice of toppings and condiments.

The suggested order for layering Beef Olé is:
Make a bed of chips on your plate, then top with meat sauce, grated cheese, shredded lettuce, chopped tomatoes, sour cream, and salsa.

PUMPKIN CURRY SOUP

SERVES	PREP	READY IN
6-8	15 minutes	40 minutes

I always double this recipe because we love it and we love to share it.

STEPS

- In 4-qt pot over medium heat, make a roux from butter, flour, and curry powder. Add a bit of the broth if needed to make a smooth paste.
- Gradually whisk in all the broth, and cook until thickened.
- Stir in pumpkin, half-and-half, and milk.
- Season with soy sauce, sugar, salt, and pepper.
- Garnish with toasted pumpkin seeds (recipe, p. 41).

INGREDIENTS

2 Tbsp butter

4 Tbsp flour

2 Tbsp curry powder

4 cups vegetable or chicken broth

3½ cups freshly puréed pumpkin (recipe, p. 41) or 29-oz can of solid packed pumpkin

¾ cup half-and-half

¾ cup milk (skim or other)

2 Tbsp soy sauce

1 Tbsp sugar

salt and pepper to taste

"Great fall dish with the right amount of spice on a cold New England day!"
—Lauren R., MA

WILD RICE AND HAM CHOWDER

SERVES
8-10

PREP
30 minutes

READY IN
1 hour

This recipe is a great way to use leftover holiday ham!

"This soup hits the spot every time!" —Betsy H., MA
(former Campbell's Chunky Soup spokesperson!)

INGREDIENTS

½ cup chopped onion

¼ cup butter, cubed

2 cloves garlic, minced

6 Tbsp flour

½ tsp salt

¼ tsp pepper

4 cups chicken broth

1½ cups cubed and peeled potatoes (or unpeeled but washed well)

½ cup chopped carrot

1 bay leaf

½ tsp dried thyme

¼ tsp nutmeg

3 cups cooked wild rice

2½ cups cubed fully cooked ham

1 cup half-and-half

1 cup milk (whole, skim, or 2%)

15.25-oz can whole kernel corn, drained (or 2 cups frozen corn)

minced fresh parsley (*for garnish*)

STEPS

- In Dutch oven, over medium heat, sauté onion in butter until tender.

- Add garlic; sauté 1 minute more.

- Stir in flour, salt, and pepper until blended.

- Gradually add broth. Bring to a boil, then cook and stir for 2 minutes or until thickened and bubbly.

- Add potatoes, carrot, bay leaf, thyme, and nutmeg; return to a boil.

- Reduce heat; cover and simmer for 30 minutes or until vegetables are tender.

- Stir in the rice, ham, half-and-half, milk, and corn; heat through (do not boil).

- Discard bay leaf. Garnish with parsley.

CHEDDAR CHOWDER

SERVES 6-8 **PREP** 15 minutes **READY IN** 40 minutes

Add a cup or two of chopped broccoli if you have it left over in the fridge.

INGREDIENTS

3 cups vegetable or chicken broth

4 medium potatoes, peeled and diced (or unpeeled but washed well)

1 medium onion, sliced

1 cup thinly sliced carrots

⅓ cup butter

⅓ cup flour

4 cups milk, warmed in microwave

12 oz sharp cheddar cheese, grated

STEPS

- In 4-qt pot, bring broth to a boil.
- Add potatoes, onion, and carrots. Bring back to a boil, then lower heat and simmer, covered, for 12 minutes.
- In separate 1-qt saucepan, melt butter, then whisk in flour.
- Pour butter-flour mixture into broth and vegetables, stirring constantly.
- Stir in milk, then add cheese, stirring to melt. Keep heat below medium and watch carefully, stirring until warm enough to serve. Be careful: once milk is added, the soup is vulnerable to scorching.

"Cheddar chowder is one of my go-to meals when I bring food to a family or when I host a gathering. It's delicious and filling, and who doesn't love cheese?" —Lisa F., CA

ROTISSERIE CHICKEN VEGETABLE SOUP

SERVES
8-10

PREP
40 minutes

READY IN
3 hours

"A heartwarming and nourishing soup that is best shared with family and friends."
—Richard H., MA

INGREDIENTS

1 rotisserie chicken

4 chicken bouillon cubes

4 large potatoes, diced

4 stalks celery, diced

2 medium onions, diced

4 large carrots, diced

salt and pepper to taste

STEPS

- In 8-qt pot, bring 4 quarts of water to boil.
- Bone and skin chicken; add skin, juices, and bones to pot but set meat aside.
- Simmer for 2 hours.
- Use colander to strain broth into another pot or large bowl. Pick out and set aside any meat, and discard the rest.
- Return strained broth to 8-qt pot and stir in bouillon cubes.
- Add diced potatoes, celery, onion, and carrots to broth.
- Bring to a boil, then simmer over medium heat until vegetables are soft.
- Dice chicken meat and add to soup.
- Add salt and pepper to taste.
- When chicken is heated through, serve!

GRANDMA ESSIE'S GUMBO

SERVES	PREP	READY IN
6-8	35 minutes	1 hour 45 minutes

"One of my most treasured memories is learning how to make gumbo with Grammy. Her cast-iron pot and the constant stir to make a perfect roux. Southern comfort food!" —Kari G., CA

INGREDIENTS

- **½ cup** vegetable oil
- **⅓ cup** flour
- **1 large** onion, chopped
- **1** green pepper, chopped
- **1 cup** diced celery
- **2 cups** okra, fresh or frozen, sliced into ½" pieces
- **1 lb** Andouille sausage, cut into ¼" slices
- **3** boneless chicken breasts, cut into bite-size pieces
- **6-oz can** tomato paste
- **8 cups** chicken stock (or use chicken bouillon)
- **2 cups** cooked ham, cubed
- **1 lb** raw shrimp, tails off
- salt and pepper to taste

This gets better with "age"—if there's any left!

STEPS

- Have all vegetables and meat cut before beginning.
- Make a roux: heat oil in cast-iron Dutch oven; whisk in flour until blended. Over medium heat, stir until roux is brown, ~10 mins.
- Add vegetables to roux and stir over medium heat for ~3 mins.
- Add sausage and chicken to pot and brown. Add tomato paste and chicken stock.
- Lower heat and let simmer for about an hour, stirring occasionally so it doesn't burn on the bottom.
- Just before serving, add the ham and the shrimp. Don't bring the gumbo back to a boil after adding raw shrimp or they'll get tough. They'll cook in the hot soup within 5-10 minutes.
- Serve over rice and enjoy.

CHILI CON CARNE

SERVES
10

PREP
30 minutes

READY IN
overnight + 4 hours

Nothing like a steaming bowl of chili con carne on a cold winter's day.
Add a side of cornbread, and you've got yourself a great meal.

"Delicious topped with shredded cheese!"
—Guy S., MA

INGREDIENTS

2 cups dry kidney beans

1½ lbs ground beef or turkey

2 28-oz cans whole tomatoes

1 medium onion, chopped and sautéed

3½ Tbsp chili powder (*or to taste*)

2½ tsp salt (*or to taste*)

STEPS

- The night before, soak beans in a large pot filled with water.

- At least 4 hours before serving time: drain water, rinse beans, add water to cover them by 3 inches, and bring to a boil.

- Lower heat to a simmer. The beans take at least 2 hours to soften.

- When beans are soft (but not mushy), gently drain in colander, rinse, and return to pot.

- In a skillet, brown ground meat.

- Pour off the fat.

- To the beans, stir in tomatoes, sautéed onions, chili powder, and salt.

- Add browned ground meat.

- Cover and simmer for at least 1 hour over very low heat, stirring frequently to avoid scorching the bottom.

DUMP DUMP SPRINKLE SPRINKLE

SERVES	PREP	READY IN
8-10	10 minutes	1½ hours

Delicious served over angel hair pasta.

INGREDIENTS

- **2 lbs** skinless boneless chicken breasts, cut into strips (or use chicken tenders)
- **12-oz jar** marinated artichokes
- **8-oz jar** sun-dried tomatoes with oil
- **1 envelope** Lipton dry onion soup mix
- **1 can** small black olives, drained
- **4 oz** pearl marinated fresh mozzarella balls
- **1 lb** angel hair pasta

STEPS

- Preheat oven to 350°F.
- Place chicken in 9" x 13" pan.
- *Dump* in artichokes (with juice).
- *Dump* in sun-dried tomatoes (with oil).
- *Sprinkle* dried onion soup mix over all.
- *Sprinkle* olives over all.
- Cover pan with foil.
- Bake for 1 hour, then remove from oven and carefully remove foil.
- Top with mozzarella balls, then return to oven, uncovered, for 15 minutes.
- Prepare angel hair pasta according to package directions.
- Serve over pasta. If desired, offer pesto as a topping (recipe, p. 102).

"Simple, easy, and a family favorite. A big crowd pleaser and a great meal to deliver to a friend!"
—Kelly P., MA

98

HASH BROWNS AND CHILI

SERVES
2

PREP
10 minutes

READY IN
30 minutes

This is a favorite camping breakfast, but sometimes we "act like we are camping" and enjoy it at home. Also great if you have leftover chili and/or baked potatoes.

"This recipe may not look like much, but when hashbrowns and chili are combined—especially near a campfire—it's pure magic."
—Julie J., VA

INGREDIENTS

2 medium potatoes

2 Tbsp butter

½ small onion, diced

15-oz can chili
(or 2 cups homemade chili—recipe, p. 85)

½ **cup** shredded cheese

STEPS

- Bake potatoes (microwave for 10 minutes or bake in 400°F oven for 45 minutes) until tender.

- Leaving peels on, grate potatoes and set aside.

- Melt butter in skillet over medium heat; add onion and sauté.

- Add potatoes to skillet and brown, turning occasionally.

- Meanwhile, heat chili in small saucepan.

- When potatoes are crisp, remove to a plate.

- Pour chili over potatoes and sprinkle with cheese.

- Enjoy!

SPAGHETTI

SERVES	PREP	READY IN
10-12	20 minutes	4½ hours

This recipe has evolved from our friend Cherylyn, to our daughter Kari, to our kitchen. It is very easy, and so much better than sauce from a jar. Use this sauce with Pizza Roll-Up (recipe, p. 99), with lasagna, or over any pasta.

INGREDIENTS

1 lb ground beef
1 lb Italian sausage
1 large onion, diced
2-3 cloves garlic, crushed
3 29-oz cans tomato sauce
2 6-oz cans tomato paste
2 tsp dried oregano
2 tsp dried basil
1 tsp crushed thyme
1 tsp dried rosemary
1 tsp red pepper flakes
1 tsp salt
1 tsp pepper
1 lb spaghetti

STEPS

- In large pot, brown beef, sausage, onion, and garlic. Drain fat.
- Stir in tomato sauce, tomato paste, and all herbs and seasonings.
- Simmer over low heat, covered, for 2-4 hours, stirring occasionally. Be careful not to burn the bottom. Thin with water if needed, or thicken by removing cover while simmering.
- Serve over spaghetti noodles, cooked to package directions.

SPUDS 'N' STUFF

SERVES
4

PREP
30 minutes

READY IN
30 minutes

Delicious with avocado slices and salsa!

"In our family, leftover baked potatoes always meant Spuds 'n' Stuff for breakfast the next day. Whether camping or eating at home, it's one of my favorite breakfast dishes!" —Lisa F., CA

INGREDIENTS

2 large potatoes

½ lb bacon

1 large head broccoli

2 Tbsp butter

1 medium onion, diced

¾ cup shredded cheese

salt and pepper to taste

STEPS

- Bake potatoes (microwave for 10 minutes or bake in 400°F oven for 45 minutes), then let cool (don't overbake or they will be hard to dice).

- Slice bacon into small pieces, fry in skillet, and set aside on paper towel to drain.

- Cut broccoli into florets. Cook until just done, but still crisp (microwave: steam for 3 minutes in covered bowl with a little water in the bottom; stovetop: blanch in boiling water for ~2 minutes).

- With peels left on, dice potatoes.

- Melt butter in 10" skillet over medium heat, then sauté onion.

- Add potatoes to skillet; cook until crisp.

- Stir in bacon and broccoli until heated.

- Top with cheese; salt and pepper to taste. Serve hot!

ENCHILADA CASSEROLE

SERVES 8-10 **PREP** 30 minutes **READY IN** 50 minutes

"A great way to serve an attractive, tasty, and much anticipated enchilada meal." —Joyce R, MI

INGREDIENTS

- **1-1½ lbs** ground beef (or turkey)
- **¾ cup** chopped onion
- **1½ cups** enchilada sauce
- **1½ cups** tomato sauce
- **½ cup** pure vegetable oil, for frying (but not coconut oil)
- **1 dozen** corn tortillas
- **¾ lb** cheddar cheese, grated
- **¾ cup** olives, sliced or chopped (optional)

STEPS

- Preheat oven to 350ºF. Spray a 9" x 13" baking pan with cooking spray.
- Brown meat and onions together in skillet; drain fat.
- In bowl, mix enchilada and tomato sauces.
- Spread ¼-½ cup of sauce mixture into prepared baking pan, just enough to cover bottom of pan.
- Add ¼" of oil to small (8") skillet over medium-high heat. One at a time, lightly fry each tortilla on both sides.
- Pat off any excess oil with a paper towel, then dip fried tortilla in sauce mixture.
- As you dip tortillas, place half of them in the bottom of prepared pan.
- Layer with approximately half of each of the following: first ground beef and onions, then grated cheese, then olives, and finally sauce.
- Dip and layer on remaining tortillas, then layer on other ingredients: first the ground beef and onions, then sauce, cheese, and olives.
- Bake about 20 minutes or until hot and cheese has melted.
- Serve with salsa (recipe, p. 103) and sour cream.

GREEN ENCHILADAS

SERVES
4-6

PREP
30 minutes

READY IN
1 hour

Serve these with salsa, Mexican rice, and tortilla chips for a satisfying supper!

"These enchiladas are approved by our 2-year-old! They are so delicious!" —Danielle B., TX

INGREDIENTS

2 cups shredded cooked chicken

2 cups shredded cheese, divided (Mexican blend, cheddar, or jack)

1 cup sour cream

1 tsp salt

½ tsp pepper

½ cup pure vegetable oil, for frying (but not coconut oil)

1 dozen corn tortillas

10-oz can green chile enchilada sauce

STEPS

- Preheat oven to 350°F.

- In bowl, combine chicken, **1 cup** of shredded cheese, sour cream, salt, and pepper.

- Add oil to 8" skillet to a depth of ¼". Over medium-high heat, lightly fry each tortilla on both sides.

- Put about ¼ cup chicken mixture down the center of each tortilla and roll up, placing them side-by-side in a 9" x 13" pan, seam side down.

- Pour enchilada sauce over all, then top with the remaining **1 cup** of shredded cheese.

- Bake for about 30 minutes, or until cheese on top is bubbling.

ITALIAN ZUCCHINI CRESCENT PIE

"*Italian Zucchini Crescent Pie is one of the first dishes I remember making on my own. I love the combination of the zucchini, the cheese, and the mustard!*"
—Lisa F., CA

SERVES
4-6

PREP
20 minutes

READY IN
40 minutes

INGREDIENTS

- **¼ cup** butter
- **4 cups** sliced zucchini
- **1 cup** chopped onion
- **½ cup** fresh parsley (or **2 Tbsp** dried)
- **¼ tsp** basil
- **¼ tsp** oregano
- **¼ tsp** garlic powder
- **½ tsp** salt
- **½ tsp** pepper
- **2** eggs, beaten
- **2 cups** shredded mozzarella cheese
- **8-oz can** refrigerator crescent rolls
- **2 tsp** prepared mustard

STEPS

- In skillet over medium heat, melt butter.
- Add zucchini and onions and cook for 15 minutes, stirring occasionally.
- Stir in parsley, basil, oregano, garlic powder, salt, and pepper, then remove from heat.
- Stir in eggs and cheese.
- In a 10" pie pan, form a crust with the crescent roll dough.
- Spread crust with mustard, then fill with zucchini mixture.
- Bake at 375°F for 18-20 minutes. Serve!

CHICKEN PARISIENNE

SERVES
6

PREP
15 minutes

READY IN
2 ½ hours

A tried-and-true, company-special, simple-to-prepare meal.

INGREDIENTS

6 boneless chicken breasts

2 cups sour cream

2 10.5-oz cans cream of mushroom soup

6 slices deli ham (*or use thinly sliced leftover ham*)

2 slices bacon, uncooked

dried parsley (*for garnish*)

STEPS

- Preheat oven to 300°F.
- In bowl, combine sour cream and soup.
- Line bottom of 9" x 13" glass pan with ham slices.
- Place chicken breasts over ham slices in pan.
- Top each breast with ⅓ slice of bacon.
- Pour soup mixture over all, then cover pan with foil.
- Bake for 2 hours.
- Remove from oven; place chicken pieces (along with ham and bacon) onto serving dish, then pour the sauce from the pan into a blender and liquify.
- Pour some of this gravy over the chicken, reserving the rest to serve on the side.
- Garnish with dried parsley and serve with rice.

SAVORY CHICKEN SQUARES

SERVES	PREP	READY IN
4	15 minutes	40 minutes

These crispy, flaky "pockets" are filled with the deliciousness of chicken, cream cheese, and onions. Don't underbake, but do enjoy!

INGREDIENTS

- **3 oz** cream cheese, softened
- **3 Tbsp** butter, melted, divided
- **2 cups** cooked, cubed chicken
- **2 Tbsp** milk
- **1 Tbsp** chopped onion
- **¼ tsp** salt
- **⅛ tsp** pepper
- **8-oz can** refrigerator crescent rolls
- **¾ cup** seasoned croutons, crushed

STEPS

- Preheat oven to 350°F.
- Blend cream cheese and 2 Tbsp butter together until smooth.
- Add chicken, milk, chopped onion, salt, and pepper and mix well.
- Separate crescent roll dough into four rectangles; press to seal perforations.
- Spoon ½ cup chicken mixture onto center of each rectangle.
- Pull four corners of dough to center of mixture; seal.
- Place filled squares on ungreased cookie sheet, seam side down.
- Brush tops with the remaining 1 Tbsp melted butter, then sprinkle with crushed croutons.
- Bake 18–20 minutes, until golden brown.

MEAT LOAF

SERVES
8

PREP
15 minutes

READY IN
1¼ hours

Use leftover cold meat loaf to make a yummy sandwich, dressed with dill pickles and catsup.

INGREDIENTS

2 lbs ground beef

1 cup dry bread crumbs (great use for stale bread)

¾ cup milk

1 egg, beaten

¾ cup finely diced onion

3 Tbsp catsup

1 Tbsp Worcestershire sauce

1 tsp garlic powder

1 tsp salt

1 tsp pepper

STEPS

- Preheat oven to 350°F.
- In large bowl, combine all ingredients except ground beef.
- Crumble in the beef and mix well.
- On rimmed baking sheet, shape meat mixture into an oval loaf, about 3" tall and 8" long.
- Bake ~1 hour, or until browned and cooked through.
- Serve hot with catsup or barbecue sauce on the side.

IF ONE OF YOU SAYS TO THEM, "GO IN PEACE; KEEP WARM AND WELL FED," BUT DOES NOTHING ABOUT THEIR PHYSICAL NEEDS,

what good is it?

JAMES 2:16

PULLED PORK

SERVES	PREP	READY IN
6-8	10 minutes	11-14 hours

Great as an entrée or for hot sandwiches.

"The best pulled pork, period. Perfectly balanced. Hearty flavor. My boys and I all had thirds the first time we tasted it!"
—Rob W, MA

INGREDIENTS

6-8 lb pork shoulder (or pork butt or pork roast)

4.5 oz pork dry rub

1 jar barbecue sauce (15-18 oz) (optional)

STEPS

- Rinse meat and pat dry.
- Rub the dry rub well into all sides of meat.
- Place meat on rack in roasting pan, fat side up, then cover pan with foil.
- Refrigerate for 2 hours (or overnight).
- Preheat oven to 250°F.
- Move roasting pan to oven and bake for 1½ hours per lb of meat or until meat is easily shredded with a fork.
- Remove from oven and let sit for 15-30 minutes.
- Remove foil, then cut off and discard fat.
- Using a fork (or two), shred meat.
- Serve as is, or add barbecue sauce to taste.

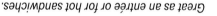

PORK RIBS

SERVES
4

PREP
5 minutes

READY IN
4-6 hours

Purchase any variety of pork ribs. The most common are baby back ribs, spare ribs, or St. Louis-style ribs.

"Amazing! Easy, tasty, tender, and juicy! These ribs turn out perfectly every time."—John N., CA

INGREDIENTS

1 full rack of pork ribs

2.5 oz pork dry rub

1 jar barbecue sauce (15–18 oz)

STEPS

- Preheat oven to 250°F. Line 9" x 13" pan with foil.

- Rinse off meat, pat dry, and rub the dry rub on both sides of ribs.

- Place in prepared pan. Cover with foil and roast ~6 hours, depending on the thickness of the rib meat. Check at 4 hours; remove from oven when meat falls off the bone. You can reheat this under the broiler if it finishes early and you're not ready to serve.

- When meat is "fall off the bone" tender, baste with your favorite barbecue sauce.

- Set oven temperature to broil, then return pan to oven for 2–3 minutes, removing as soon as the sauce starts to bubble.

- Serve hot, with extra barbecue sauce on the side.

TUNA BUNSTEADS

A great way to use up leftover hamburger buns.

SERVES	PREP	READY IN
2	10 minutes	15 minutes

INGREDIENTS

5-oz can tuna, drained (*or used chopped canned chicken*)

1 Tbsp mayonnaise

¼ tsp lemon juice

1 bun, halved and toasted

¼ cup grated cheese

STEPS

- In bowl, combine tuna, mayonnaise, and lemon juice (and anything else you like to put in tuna).
- Place opened bun on foil-lined cooking sheet and spread each half with tuna mixture.
- Top with grated cheese.
- Broil for 2–3 minutes, until cheese is bubbling—but stand watch carefully!
- Serve immediately.

THEY ALL ATE
and were satisfied
MARK 6:42

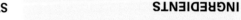

PIZZA ROLL-UP

SERVES
6-8

PREP
30 minutes

READY IN
2 ⅔ hours

I once entered this original recipe in a Pillsbury Bake-Off contest using Pillsbury's pizza dough. It was an instant hit with our family and is a favorite to this day with all our kids and grandkids.

INGREDIENTS

2 Tbsp yeast

2 cups lukewarm water

1 Tbsp sugar

1 tsp salt

2 Tbsp olive oil

3-4 cups flour

4 cups mozzarella cheese, shredded

8 oz pepperoni, thinly sliced (*or cooked ground sausage*)

Optional additions: mushrooms, sliced bell peppers, chopped onions, chopped ham and pineapple, *or any other pizza toppings*

STEPS

- In large bowl, dissolve yeast in lukewarm water.

- Stir in sugar, salt, and olive oil.

- Mix in flour. Add more flour as needed to make a medium-soft dough.

- Turn out onto floured surface and knead until smooth and elastic.

- Place dough in greased bowl; cover and let rise in a warm place until doubled in size (~1 hour).

- Divide dough into two equal pieces (about 1 lb 2 oz each) and roll each piece into a 10" x 16" rectangle, long edge toward you.

- Sprinkle each rectangle with half the shredded cheese and pepperoni or sausage—including any additional toppings (sautéed a bit to soften, as needed).

- Roll up tightly from long edge and pinch together to seal roll.

- Place each 16" roll on a cookie sheet and let rise for ~30 mins.

- Bake at 370°F for ~30 minutes.

- Let stand about 10 minutes then cut in 1½" slices.

- Serve with hot spaghetti sauce (recipe, p. 88) as a topping.

Dressings and Sauces

SPICE IS NICE

WHEN YOU HAVE EATEN AND ARE SATISFIED,
PRAISE THE LORD YOUR GOD FOR THE GOOD LAND
HE HAS GIVEN YOU. —DEUTERONOMY 8:10

PESTO ALBERTO

MAKES	PREP	READY IN
2 cups	15 minutes	15 minutes

Serve at room temperature, tossed with hot pasta or on sliced tomatoes.
This is also great with turkey or chicken, or on hamburgers!

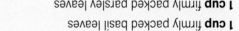

INGREDIENTS

1 cup firmly packed basil leaves

1 cup firmly packed parsley leaves

½ cup walnuts *(or pine nuts)*

½ cup freshly grated Parmesan cheese

6 small cloves garlic

1 cup olive oil

salt and pepper to taste

additional olive oil, as needed

STEPS

- In blender, put herbs, nuts, cheese, and garlic.
- With motor running, add olive oil in a stream and blend until smooth.
- Season with salt and pepper.
- Add more olive oil as needed to thin to desired consistency.
- Store refrigerated in a covered glass container, or freeze in ice cube tray (and then bag the cubes).

SALSA

MAKES
2 quarts

PREP
20 minutes

READY IN
20 minutes

INGREDIENTS

1 jalapeño pepper

1 Hungarian pepper *(yellow)*

1 serrano pepper

3 cloves garlic

1 bunch cilantro

28 oz diced tomatoes, drained

28 oz tomato sauce

1 Tbsp Worcestershire sauce

salt and pepper to taste

This makes a fairly spicy salsa, but you can adjust the heat by adding or deleting peppers. Serranos are the most spicy, followed by jalapeños and then Hungarian.

STEPS

- Cut peppers in half and cook with garlic in skillet using medium heat until darkly roasted.
- Chop pepper mixture and put in blender or food processor.
- Chop one bunch of cilantro and blend.
- Add diced tomatoes, tomato sauce, Worcestershire sauce, salt, and pepper.
- Blend and enjoy!

Passed down to our son-in-law Gabe from his Uncle Mike, and then on to us. Our grandson Nathan loves Papa's salsa. To him a chip is just a vehicle to transport salsa to his mouth; he has been known to consume a pint of salsa at one sitting. Consume with care.

DEREK'S SALAD DRESSING

MAKES ¾ cup
PREP 10 minutes
READY IN 20 minutes

Delicious on a green salad!

INGREDIENTS

- ½ **cup** olive oil
- 1 **tsp** Dijon mustard
- dash of salt
- juice of ½ lemon
- 1 **clove** garlic

STEPS

- Grate garlic with a microplaner.
- In bowl, mix grated garlic, lemon juice, and salt.
- Let sit for 10 minutes.
- Add mustard, then drizzle in oil while whisking to emulsify.

KOREAN BBQ TERIYAKI MARINADE

MAKES 1¼ cups
PREP 5 minutes
READY IN 5 minutes

This makes enough for ~2 lbs of meat. Good on chicken, ribs, London broil, flank steak strips, chuck roast, and more!

Best when used on meat cooked on a BBQ grill, but also great when cooking in the oven.

INGREDIENTS

- ½ **cup** soy sauce
- ¼ **cup** sherry
- ¼ **cup** pure vegetable oil
- ¼ **cup** finely diced onion
- 2 **tsp** finely minced garlic
- 1 **tsp** finely grated ginger
- 1 **Tbsp** sugar
- ½ **tsp** pepper

STEPS

- Whisk together all ingredients.
- Marinate meat overnight.
- Grill!

SECRET SAUCE

MAKES
4 cups

PREP
5 minutes

READY IN
5 minutes

A great sauce for dipping artichokes, as well as for putting on hamburgers and fries.

INGREDIENTS

1 quart mayonnaise

1 Tbsp puréed garlic

½ cup lemon juice

¾ tsp paprika

1 Tbsp minced parsley

STEPS

- Mix all ingredients and enjoy!
- Store any leftovers in the refrigerator for up to 1 week.

TARTAR SAUCE

MAKES
1 cup

PREP
5 minutes

READY IN
5 minutes

Delicious on fried fish, clams, and fish sandwiches!

INGREDIENTS

½ cup mayonnaise

½ cup sour cream

1 dill pickle, finely diced

1 Tbsp finely diced onion

dill pickle juice to taste

STEPS

- Mix all ingredients and enjoy!
- Store any leftovers in the refrigerator for up to 1 week.

BLUEBERRY SAUCE

MAKES
2 cups

PREP
10 minutes

READY IN
20 minutes

INGREDIENTS

2 Tbsp cornstarch

1 cup water, divided

½ cup sugar

3 Tbsp fresh lemon juice

2 cups blueberries (fresh or frozen)

½ tsp cinnamon

STEPS

- In 1-qt saucepan, dissolve cornstarch in ¼ cup water.
- Add remaining ¾ cup water, sugar, and lemon juice.
- Stir over medium heat until it begins to thicken.
- Add blueberries and cinnamon, and cook while stirring (about 5 minutes) until the sauce thickens and covers the back of the spoon.
- Remove from heat and let cool about 10 minutes.
- Serve with hot pancakes!

with glad and generous hearts

AND DAY BY DAY, ATTENDING
THE TEMPLE TOGETHER
AND BREAKING BREAD
IN THEIR HOMES, THEY
RECEIVED THEIR FOOD

ACTS 2:46

RASPBERRY COMPOTE

MAKES
2 cups

PREP
10 minutes

READY IN
20 minutes

Delicious on pancakes or waffles—and superb over ice cream or on cheesecake.

INGREDIENTS

1 Tbsp cornstarch

4 Tbsp water

2 cups fresh or frozen raspberries

2 Tbsp sugar

1 Tbsp lemon juice

STEPS

- Dissolve cornstarch in water.
- In saucepan over medium heat, combine dissolved cornstarch, raspberries, sugar, and lemon juice.
- Bring to boil and allow to boil for about 5 minutes, stirring constantly.
- Reduce heat to low and let simmer for 10 minutes.
- Serve hot with pancakes or waffles.
- Store in refrigerator for up to 1 week, or in freezer for up to 6 months.

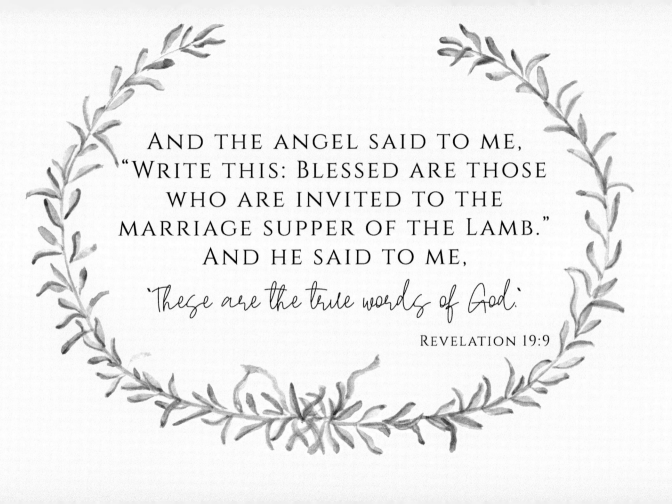

And the angel said to me,
"Write this: Blessed are those
who are invited to the
marriage supper of the Lamb."
And he said to me,

These are the true words of God.

Revelation 19:9

COOKS' NOTES

T hough baking and cooking use mathematics, they certainly are not exact sciences. We have attempted to take as much ambiguity out of the recipes as possible, but with that said, don't be anxious if you don't have a pinch of this or that. As you use these recipes, keep in mind that there are many variables at play. Every oven is different—in one oven, cookies bake at 375 degrees for 12 minutes, and in another, for 15 minutes. Your package of meat may not be the exact weight called for, the ribs may not quite fit the pan called for, and the yield of cookies may be more or less depending on how well you have packed the dough into your cookie scoop. Feel free to adjust and don't sweat the "non-exact" aspects of cooking—just enjoy the experience and the results.

O ne other conviction and challenge we offer regarding food and its many uses: thoughtfully consider how to minimize waste by exercising good stewardship principles. Living in the "land of plenty," one can so easily "waste" excess. Over the years of our culinary history together, we have discovered great delight and creativity in "repurposing" leftover food, choosing to fill our bellies rather than our trash cans. For example, stale bread can be refashioned into croutons or bread crumbs (e.g., for the meat loaf recipe). Leftover baked potatoes can become an ingredient in *Spuds 'n' Stuff* or *Hash Browns and Chili*. Fruit that's "on the edge" can inspire delicious smoothies. We invite you to engage in the Great Adventure of stewarding well God's generous gift of food.

Baked potatoes: When we're baking potatoes, we often throw in a few extra so we can make *Spuds 'n' Stuff or Hash Browns and Chili* the next day.

Baking soda: When using baking soda in a recipe, we always "sift" it through a small wire strainer to avoid a lump of soda showing up in the final product.

Beans: 1 lb of beans is 2 cups; cooked, they yield 6 cups of beans.

Berries: When fresh berries are in season and less expensive, we stock up and fill our freezer. To avoid gallon-size bags of solid mass, we "*Individually Quick Freeze*" (IQF) the fruit: After cleaning the berries and letting them dry on paper towels, spread them out on a rimmed baking sheet, single layer, and freeze. Scoop the frozen berries into a ziplock bag and return to freezer. When you need a cup of berries, it's easy to get one cup from the bag of IQF berries. Blueberries, raspberries, and strawberries are great candidates for this process.

Breads: If you're not going to use your fresh bread within a couple of days, slice the loaf and freeze it. Then you can easily take out any number of slices as needed.

Lemons: When the tree is burgeoning with delicious ripe lemons that outpace your ability to completely consume or give away, "shave" the zest with a microplaner and freeze for future use. Then juice the lemons, freeze the juice in ice cube trays, then pop the cubes into a ziplock bag and return to freezer to have fresh lemon juice year-round.

Pesto: When basil is plentiful, we make pesto and freeze it in ice cube trays. After it's frozen, bag the cubes and keep them in the freezer, taking out enough to make meals with all winter long. The cubes don't take long to thaw at room temperature, and voilà—you're good to go.

Scones: The sliced dough can be frozen pre-baked, "IQF," as for berries, above. Let thaw at room temperature when you're ready to use them and bake and frost as instructed. Fresh-baked scones on short notice!

Sour milk: Don't throw it away! Keep it in the refrigerator, but **mark it** as sour, to prevent unsuspecting humans who live in your house from pouring a glass. Use it in *Cowboy Coffee Cake* or *Baked Brown Bread*.

RESOURCES

Parenting Resources

Raising a Trailblazer, Virginia Friesen.
Parenting by Design, Paul and Virginia Friesen. (DVD)
The Father's Heart, Paul and Virginia Friesen. (DVD)

Dating and Engagement

Letters to My Daughters, Paul Friesen.
Letters to My Daughters Discussion Guide, Paul Friesen
Before You Save the Date, Paul Friesen.
So You Want to Marry My Daughter?, Paul Friesen.
Engagement Matters, Paul and Virginia Friesen. (study guide)

Marriage

The Marriage App, Paul and Virginia Friesen.
Restoring the Fallen, Earl and Sandy Wilson, Paul and Virginia Friesen, Larry and Nancy Paulson.
Marriage, Culture, and Scripture, Paul and Virginia Friesen.
In Our Image, Paul and Virginia Friesen. (study guide)
Jesus on Marriage, Paul and Virginia Friesen. (study guide)
Recapturing Eden, Paul and Virginia Friesen. (DVD)
Created in God's Image, Paul and Virginia Friesen. (DVD)
The Delight of Sacrificial Love in Marriage, Paul and Virginia Friesen. (CD)
The Delight of Experiencing Love and Respect in Marriage, Paul and Virginia Friesen. (CD)
The Delight of Uniqueness in Marriage, Paul and Virginia Friesen. (CD)
The Delight of Sexual Intimacy in Marriage, Paul and Virginia Friesen. (CD)

For details on these and other H.I.M. resources, visit:
www.HIMweb.org

ABOUT THE AUTHORS

Drs. Paul and Virginia Friesen have been involved in Family Ministries for more than 40 years through family camps, church staff positions, speaking, consulting, and writing. In 2003, they founded Home Improvement Ministries (www.HIMweb.org), a non-profit organization dedicated to equipping individuals and churches to better encourage marriages and families in living out God's design for healthy relationships.

As the lead resource couple at Home Improvement Ministries, the Friesens regularly speak at marriage, men's, and women's conferences in the US and internationally, as well as local family and parenting seminars, and have an ongoing ministry with professional athletes. Paul and Virginia both have doctorates in Marriage and Family Therapy from Gordon-Conwell Theological Seminary.

Between them they have authored more than fifteen books and curriculums on parenting and marriage, including *Letters to My Daughters*, *In Our Image*, *Raising a Trailblazer*, *Before You*

Save the Date, *The Marriage App*, and most recently, *Lovin' Your Wife Like Christ When You Ain't No Jesus*.

Paul and Virginia were married in 1976 and are the parents of three young adult women, two of whom are now married to wonderful, godly men. Their middle daughter is living fully for Christ as a single woman and trusting God for His best. Paul and Virginia's greatest joy in life is knowing that their children are "walking in the truth."

INDEX